Sligachan

Camasunary

Arthur R. Griffith.

The Cuillin from Portree

THE CUILLIN
OF SKYE

by

B. H. Humble

THE ERNEST PRESS

First published 1952
Facsimile edition 1986
Copyright © Dr. R. M. Humble

To Jock and Davie
and howffing days

Humble, B.H.
  The Cuillin of Skye.
  1. Mountaineering — Scotland — Black Cuillin (Skye) — History
  2. Black Cuillin (Skye) — History
  I. Title
  796.5'22'0941182   GV199.44.G72B5

ISBN 0–948153–01–6

Graphic origination by Arneg, Glasgow
Printed by M & A Thomson, East Kilbride
Bound by Hunter & Foulis, Edinburgh

Contents

Contents

Illustrations

Illustrations

The above illustrations numbered 8, 40–47 and 50 are reproduced from photographs supplied by Guy Barlow; 13, 14, 18, 19, 24, 35, 37, 38, 39 and 49 by G. P. Abraham; 29, 30, 31 and 36 by W. Douglas; 2, 9 and 12 by R. M. Adam; 6, 55 and 56 by H. Restall; 17, 22 and 71 by D. Easson; 51 and 52 by Penelope Poulton; the frontispiece by Robert McLean; 1 by W.W. Weir, F.R.P.S.; 16 by Lafosse, 21 by A. E. Robertson; 48 by A. H. Doughty; 53 by W. E. Ball, A.R.P.S.; 54 by Ian W. Craig, A.R.P.S.; 60 by A. M. Smith; 63 by R. Anderson; 66 by D. Scott, and 73 by C. M. Dixon.

Numbers 7, 10, 15, 20, 23, 25, 27, 32, 33, 34, 57, 58, 59, 61, 62, 64, 65, 67–70 and 72 are from the author's own collection.

Illustration number 3 is reproduced from a painting by George Fennel Robson; 4 from a sketch by J. M. W. Turner and 5 from a sketch by an unknown artist.

Acknowledgments

MY grateful thanks are due to members of many Mountaineering Clubs who gave me information, and particularly to:

The Editor of the *Scottish Mountaineering Club Journal*, for permission to use material relating to Skye which has appeared therein and for the loan of two old blocks.

The Editors of the *Fell and Rock Club Journal*, the *Pinnacle Club Journal* and Dr. Mabel Barker for information relating to women climbers in Skye.

The Secretaries of the Climbers' Club, Fell and Rock Club, Midland Association of Mountaineers, Wayfarer's Club and Yorkshire Ramblers for information as to main ridge traverses by their members and to the many individuals who wrote me about this matter.

The Editor of the *Alpine Journal* and the Executors of the late Norman Collie, Clinton Dent and Charles Pilkington for quotations from their articles.

The Executors of the late A. P. Abraham for quotations from *Rock Climbing in Skye*.

The Executors of the late J. E. B. Wright and the Moray Press for quotation from *Mountain Days in the Isle of Skye*.

The Executors of the late Richard Hillary and Macmillan & Co. Ltd. for quotation from *The Last Enemy*.

The Director of the Victoria and Albert Museum, South Kensington, for permission to reproduce G. F. Robson's "Loch Coruisk".

Mr Alex. Small and Mr D. D. Stewart for help with the climbing routes on photos 32–34 and to the latter for information regarding the latest new climbs.

Mr Ian Campbell of Sligachan Hotel, Mr John Campbell of Cuillin Cottage, Mr Ewen MacRae of Glen Brittle House and Miss Chisholm of Glen Brittle Post Office for putting their Visitors' and Climbers' Books at my disposal.

Mr John Dunlop of the Mitchell Library, Glasgow, and Mr. G. C. Williams, Honorary Librarian of the Scottish Mountaineering Club, for help in tracing obscure references.

Mr. T. M. Wedderburn for information regarding war-time training in Skye.

All whose photographs appear in this book and all others who answered my queries.

Arthur R. Griffiths for the map, line sketches and diagrams.

Finally to Dr Guy Barlow, who proved a fount of information as to the 1900–1924 period and who helped to check the proofs, and to Dr I. M. M. MacPhail, who looked over the original typescript and the final proofs, made many valuable suggestions and gave much help as to Gaelic spelling.

COMELY BANK,
  DUMBARTON.
   June 1952.

Introduction

IT was our first visit to Skye and we were walking round the island. In the late afternoon of the second day we reached the little village of Sconser. We were tired and footsore and did not feel like continuing to Sligachan, three miles further on, so hoped that Sconser would provide a lodging for the night.

It did not promise much, for the village consists only of a few crofts under the shadow of Glamaig. On enquiry we were told to try Mackenzie's cottage and were directed there. It contained only a room and kitchen (a but and ben) and a loft reached by a ladder.

We were at once given the room for the night and were soon sitting down to a substantial high tea at the window. It was then that I noticed a big pile of *Alpine Club Journals* in a corner and puzzled over the possible connection between the Alpine Club and that little croft in a remote corner of Skye. The Journals seemed quite out of place.

Later, as we sat outside, a man came up from the road towards the croft. And what a man! He was an old man, yet walked easily and his eyes were clear. That grand white beard would have made him notable in any company. He wore an ancient suit of plus fours, big heavy boots, a deer-stalker cap and carried some trout. We were invited into the kitchen and sat round the fire in the gloaming. The old man's interest was aroused when we told him we hoped to climb one of the Cuillin peaks the following week. Obviously he knew them well, for, instead of talking of danger and difficulty as most folk would have done, he said that Sgurr Alasdair, the highest of them all, was "just a walk, just a walk". He showed us many old photographs of rock climbing and a series of stereoscopic views. There seemed to be nothing about the Cuillin which he did not know.

We had gathered by this time that he himself was a guide to the Cuillin and that he had spent the day fishing in Loch Fada with Professor Collie. The names Mackenzie and Collie did not signify anything to us, for we knew nothing of mountains or mountaineering. It was late when we went to bed, and though we were at breakfast by eight Mackenzie had already gone off for a day's fishing somewhere.

We walked on to Portree, and it was that talk about the mountains which made us leave the road. If an old man of seventy could walk to the highest Cuillin surely we could climb the Storr, which looked quite easy. We did more than that. We walked from Portree to Staffin via the Storr and the intervening hills. For tyros with big packs who knew nothing of hill walking that is quite a hefty undertaking.

Later we climbed our peak of the Cuillin; we saw our first rock climbers; we found a copy of the Scottish Mountaineering Club Guide to Skye at Glen Brittle and learned of the existence of that club. But it was not till I returned to Glasgow, haunted the library and read everything I could find about Skye that I fully appreciated how lucky we were falling in with John Mackenzie that night at Sconser.

We had stepped into an unknown croft in Skye and met "the only mountain guide of Swiss calibre Britain had ever produced" and who, that day, had been in the company of a world-famous mountaineer, the two of them, long years ago, having ushered in the Golden Age of climbing in Skye!

The mystery of the *Alpine Journals* was cleared up. For John Mackenzie, though he never climbed in the Alps, was made a sort of honorary member of that club and received the Journal regularly in appreciation of his great services to British Mountaineering.

Mackenzie and Collie were continual companions in their later years, and when John died in 1934 Collie wrote of him:

> "No one knew the Cuillin better than John Mackenzie. Many are the best climbs he was the first to accomplish; he was the first to set foot on A'Chioch in Coire Lagan, a spot that may now be described as the Mecca of British climbers. As a companion on a long summer day he was perfect. Always cheerful, keenly alive to everything—the wild birds, the fish in the rivers, the deer on the hillside, and all natural things.
>
> There is no one who can take his place. Those who knew him will remember him a perfect gentleman, one who never offended either by word or deed. He has left a gap that cannot be filled. There was only one John, simple-minded, most lovable and without guile. May he rest quietly in the little graveyard at Struan."

xi

Collie himself took part in great first ascents in Norway, in the Canadian Rockies, in the Alps and in the Himalaya, and was the last to bid farewell to Mummery before that desperate assault of Nanga Parbat, yet the Cuillin of Skye were his greatest love. He went to Sligachan to live in 1939 and died there in 1942 at the age of eighty-four.

Richard Hillary, one of the Battle of Britain pilots, whose book *The Last Enemy* is one of the few great books of the War, spent a leave in Skye in 1940, and gave us a last picture of Collie:

> "We were alone in the inn save for one old man who had returned there to die. His hair was white but his face and bearing were those of a mountaineer, though he must have been a great age. He never spoke, but appeared regularly at meals to take his place at a table tight pressed against a window, alone with his wine and his memories. We thought him rather fine."

I found another link with the Golden Age in correspondence with Lawrence Pilkington over the last years of his life. For Lawrence, with his brother Charles, made the first ascent of the Inaccessible Pinnacle of Sgurr Dearg in 1880. He lived to the age of eighty-six and his letters, in perfect copper-plate throughout, are full of love of the hills. He wrote of his last view of Skye, from the top of the Mam Ratagan road—"a glimpse of the promised land".

Skye is the only place in Scotland where mountains are named after men. Hoary names they have—Sgurr Alasdair, Sgurr Thearlaich, Sgurr Thormaid and Sgurr Mhic Coinnich. And never were men more worthy of giving their names to mountains than Sheriff Nicolson, Charles Pilkington, Norman Collie and John Mackenzie.

Formerly Skye was the haunt of the select few and accommodation difficult to come by. Now thousands climb in Skye; no one can really call himself a British mountaineer who has not climbed in Skye. There is treasure among the Cuillin. Here is the story of those who have gone to find it.

Foreword

By W.H. MURRAY

Ben Humble was born at Dumbarton in 1904, one of eight brothers. The more important point to know about Ben is that here was a youth of bright mind, force of personality, and vigour of body, who on leaving Glasgow High School had his hopes frustrated by a fast-growing deafness. The experience induced later eccentricities and a stubborn will — both to be turned to the benefit of others.

Ben graduated in dental surgery at Glasgow. His student days were made harder by his own refusal to acknowledge lost hearing. In hope of recovery, he declined to lip-read. His mother tried to persuade him but told me that Ben would not even begin to learn. Archie MacAlpine, his fellow student at dental college, told me too that Ben spent a whole term carving his name three inches high on his desk, for he felt obliged to sit out lectures hearing nothing. Undaunted, he duly set up in general practice, from which he withdrew in 1935 to specialize in radiology. Dentists then rarely had X-ray machines, but even so found communication with Ben too hard. He was now stone deaf, and by 1937 had abandoned dentistry to earn a living from journalism, photography, and books — a market he had entered four years previously. For a short while he was editor of Scotland's first hill-walkers' magazine *Open Air in Scotland* (1945-49), but that died when it failed to attract advertisers. Ben survived with apparent ease. He was an alert, hard-headed business man who knew how to drive bargains, yet a vast amount of his time and energy went to voluntary interests, mostly profitless in money-terms, and far beyond what other and lesser mortals could possibly sustain. Ben roused in me, and all who knew him, wonder and admiration. We could not imagine how he made the time or kept the pace. One thing is certain, he was driven, positively driven by deafness into a need of constant communication and perpetual involvement in affairs.

When I first met Ben, his principal activities (apart from radiology) were mountaineering in all its branches; cross-country running with Dumbarton Harriers (he was an early organizer of the annual race up Ben Nevis); botany, in which he was expert on heathers; photography, extending in early days to movies when he filmed an ascent of the Cobbler's South Peak; and public speaking through membership of a dining club, so that despite peculiarities of accent caused by deafness he became a top-class after-dinner speaker, able to combine a fluent wit with good sense. These were only some of his interests, each and all pursued with infectious enthusiasm.

Ben had walked the hills from his youth, and began rock and snow climbing when he joined the Junior Mountaineering Club of Scotland in 1930. Our introduction came at a club lecture in Glasgow in 1935. He was short in stature, with alert brown eyes that often held a mischievous gleam; his hair was already thinning to baldness. I was only 22, an age at which men of 30 are believed to have one foot in the grave, yet with Ben this thought never occurred to me. A natural vitality made him ageless.

I had no thought of climbing with Ben until June the following year, when chance brought our tents to the same camp-site at Glen Brittle in Skye. I discovered there that the hard-headed Ben was a whole-hearted romantic, to whom the mountain ambience was all and physical discomforts nothing — a too rare quality that made him for me instantly congenial company. The first intimation came at 10 o'clock one evening, when I stood outside to watch the mist gather and swirl round the Cuillin. His head suddenly thrust from the door of his tent. "It would be a fine night for a climb", he announced, and I knew from his voice that he meant it. The notion startled me. I was a beginner. Night climbing had not yet entered my dreams. "We'd start right now," he added, "up to the main ridge, north along the tops — aaaaaah" I protested the need of food and sleep, this to express a merely bodily wish, for the mind was already aloft. We left within minutes, and enjoyed the best night and morning we were ever to have in Skye, finishing down at Coruisk.

I revert to Ben's long-drawn *aaaaaah* — an habitual expression. By subtle inflexion of voice he could use it to signify equally well approval or censure, or to convey from the gamut of emotion any note that he chose — delight, derision, admiration, contempt, laughter, scepticism, wonder, scandal, irony — all unaffectedly since he could hear nothing of his own tone, giving unerring expression to inward feeling. His eloquent *aaaaaahs* could communicate more than other men's innumerable words.

Ben and I climbed often together in 1936 and 1937, but rarely on rock above *very difficult* standard. On severe rock his deafness affected balance, and communication became too chancy (unless on a short climb). For this reason he never led difficult routes. He was competent and never came off. In August 1937, he and I accounted for all the known Cobbler climbs in 7 hours on wet rock, starting at 1 pm when the rain stopped. (In these days there were less than twenty routes). In wider fields he was a thoroughly good mountaineer.

I found his photography a sore trial of my patience. He was so keen, his eye so constantly given to the endless search for dramatic stances, unusual lighting, right composition, revealing effects, that hours would seem to go while we dilly-dallied. I learned more patience when I viewed the results. Perhaps the best reward we had, since it yielded his best-known and favourite picture, came from one trying hour in June 1936, spent in posing me on the Cioch Pinnacle. The time was 9 pm and broad daylight with a cloud-sea below, yet by judicious stopping of the camera he created a splendid sunset photograph, in which Nature was lent a helping hand, yet all was true to the Cuillin at their best. To me that seemed good art, and justified (See Plate 69). His hunger for good subjects did make him on occasion quite unscrupulous, as witness the day I came down from the rocks to our camp in Glen Brittle, and found Ben absorbed in photographing a cow, which was munching my pyjamas where they hung on a drying-line. I raged. Ben was totally unrepentant. His image stays with me, face gleeful, an imp of mischief.

The real Ben came out in his love of highly uncomfortable howffs. Often he would bicycle up from Dumbarton to Arrochar to sleep in the caves of Ben Narnain, or else at the Narnain Boulder under the Cobbler corrie. He records a night at the Boulder when "after midnight we watched moonset. It gave out diffuse rays and lit up the whole corrie so that familiar shapes became unreal; then as it slowly disappeared beneath the ridge darkness came once more. We were up with the dawn.

By 7 the leader had started on the first pitch."

Ben was devoted to the Cobbler, and to Arrochar, where he lived for many years, and to the gentle art of howffing for which that district lavishly provides. He writes of one New Year howff, 1600 feet up on Beinn an Lochain:

"I was particularly anxious to test this one under hard conditions as it had been my own discovery the previous April — still do I remember the sunset over distant Loch Fyne, perfectly framed in the arch which formed the entrance, and named the howff 'Sunset Arch'. We had hoped for really frosty conditions at New Year, but typical Arrochar rain was our reward. When heavy rain came in drips from the roof, it was a queer business sitting round a blazing fire wearing oilskins. Our preoccupation was such that no one noticed candle-grease steadily dripping into the pan of soup hottering up, till at last the candle itself fell in." (No change to the flavour).

"Always," he continues, "we hankered for a cave under real winter conditions," and at last he found both at a Hogmanay howff in the Lost Valley of Glen Coe. "My brightest memory is of sallying forth in the deep snow, returning with two armfuls of icicles and discovering that porridge made from icicles was much better than porridge made from snow. Conditions that night had been just about as severe as could be experienced in Scotland."

Much of his howffing had been done in Jock Nimlin's company. He used to quote with relish Nimlin's opinion that howffing ought to be an essential part of the climbing game, which might eliminate some of the dross from mountaineering clubs. "All members of the SMC" (Ben had joined in 1936) "should be let loose in a high corrie one winter evening, each to find his own howff, those present in the morning to remain members — aaaaaah!"

I could not wholly agree with Ben on howffs. I thought a tent pitched high on the mountains was a lighter and more cheerful place than a rock cave. But Ben would have none of that: "Mountain camping is all very well, but the inside of a tent is always the same and once in there is nothing to do. Each howff is different, each has its building problems, each its own charm, each its own memories. And there is always so much to do, for howffing refinements are endless." Ben had always this need to be up and doing, an affliction that never unduly troubled me.

Above: *The Humble Kipper* (see page xvi) photographed in Glen Brittle by A.M. MacAlpine in the late 1930's. The insert shows Ben Humble much later in life after having received the MBE in recognition of his lifetime's service to Mountain Rescue.

Over: Ben Humble in Iceland, 1930.   Photo: Douglas Scott

Disputes with Ben were frequent and long pursued. Always he had the last word. Nearly all trouble arose from some written note. He kept a notebook for companions to write down their thoughts or replies. Ben's advantage then was this permanent record of everything that everyone ever said, often in unwise haste. He could refer back and confound the man who had changed an opinion or a lightly given promise. But the real ground of trouble was that written words so often fail to convey the full meaning of words uttered — the tone of voice is absent. In speech one can say without offence to a hearing person many things that written would arouse wrath. One may speak frankly if the tone is heard to be friendly, or concerned, or humorous. When young I would sometimes forget this in the heat of the moment when scribbling a note to Ben — as did most people sooner or later — forget too, since Ben himself was most outspoken, that he was far more sensitive to our adverse opinions than we to his, and Ben, misinterpreting, would then feel grossly insulted.

My worst offence came when I was organizing in Glasgow a photographic exhibition for the JMCS. Archie MacAlpine submitted a print of Ben sitting outside his tent in Glen Brittle eating a kipper. He looked the picture of an old tramp and the entry was titled *The Humble Kipper*. It gave me delight — a riposte too for that cow-and-pyjamas photo. When Ben came into the room and saw it, he ripped it off the wall. I asked for his notebook and wrote, "Don't be a b-f- please put it back." His fury boiled over. He would neither speak to me nor see me again for nearly two years, in which time war had broken out. The next time we met was by chance in the summer of 1945 in Sauchiehall Street. He came up to me grinning, "Three years in prison camps — aaaaaah! — maybe you've been punished enough," and held out his hand, which I thankfully took.

Thereafter Ben made me work on his latest ploy. In 1945 he had turned his energies to mountain rescue, which from 1936 had been organized by a committee drawn from the mountaineering clubs and named the *Mountain Safety Committee*. Ben had been involved from the start. With his usual clear-headedness he now foresaw the rise in climbers' numbers and the coming need for locally raised teams to take over the physical task of rescue from the clubs, while the central committee concentrated on fostering mountain safety by propaganda, and by negotiating support from public authorities, central and local. I and others were persuaded too and the result was the formation in 1945 of the *Mountain Rescue Committee for Scotland*. By 1950 the local teams had been raised, and in that year, under the chairmanship of Donald Duff, the well-known surgeon, the new regime was finally established. Ben was a member of committee and made two most important contributions: first, his fight to ensure that control remained with the mountaineers and did not fall to a statutory body, like the Police; and second, his recording of mountain accidents over the next 32 years of his life, starting from 1945. No one with less than Ben's strong will, maintained over the years, could have extracted all the information required from reluctant teams, who had no liking for files and reports, until at last reporting became habitual. The result was an invaluable fund of rescue and safety data, which he was determined to use positively. His theme on committee was that while the teams' job was to save life, the Committee's job was to prevent accidents. To that end he pioneered the Duff Memorial Mountain Safety Exhibition, *Adventure in Safety*, held in Glasgow in 1968, and subsequently in London, Edinburgh, Aberdeen, and Fort William. It became a permanent, transportable exhibition, which showed great numbers of young hill-walkers how best to enjoy mountains. In 1972 he received an MBE.

In achieving his multitudinous ends, Ben became a thorn in the flesh of every dilatory office-bearer, editor, or committee man, a constant spur to the most active, and to all his friends a fount of advice that poured out of him in a daily stream of correspondence. We all had to keep special files for Ben alone. He seemed to know everything and everyone, deafness no handicap at all. In the mountain fraternity, Ben was the best informed man, to whom everyone could turn for the latest, most accurate, inside information. Even at the general meetings of any society or club, he could not only take part in debates, working from brief notes passed by friends, but had the most bewildering instinct for knowing instantly what had been said in response, when he would jump to his feet and rout an opponent. This happened so often that I began to doubt his deafness, which I at last tested (out of doors) by blowing a police whistle behind his head — and Ben was indeed stone deaf.

Being more alert and brighter minded than his friends and (temporary) enemies, Ben could be quite excessively irritating: when we rejected his sage advices he almost always proved to be right — nor did he fail to remind us of that at the end, when his trumpeted *aaaaaah!* rang in our ears.

Ben somehow made time to write six books. The first in 1933 was *Tramping in Skye*, the scene of his early walking — in 1930 he had helped to organize the first *Skye Week*. It has been said that Arrochar was Ben's spiritual home, but the same could be said of Skye or the Cairngorms, or wherever else he happened to be. He had already begun to build his anthology of 70 poems, which he published in 1936 as *The Songs of Skye*. The first nine publishers had turned it down — enough to deter anyone but Ben. "There's no sale for poetry" they rightly told him. But the tenth had faith and sold four editions in twenty years. A third book, *Wayfaring around Scotland*, I never saw. His first book of photographs *On Scottish Hills* was well-timed for 1946. I noted that not one of his 75 prints showed the Cuillin. That could mean only one thing — a book in the offing. We had to wait six years for it, while he researched and earned a living by journalism, public lecture tours, and production of six booklets for the tourist trade, together with picture post-cards from his own photographs. *The Cuillin of Skye* at last appeared in 1952, published by Hale. This was by far Ben's best book and unique in its subject, a history of the Cuillin with over 70 photographs, of which nearly a third were his own. Last of all came his guide-book, *Rock Climbs at Arrochar*, written with Jock Nimlin and published by the SMC in 1954.

Ben had another gift that all might envy, an instinctive rapport with children. They responded, liking him instantly. The best in Ben came out in their company. He sparkled and all his cares fell away. When the first Adventure Centre opened at Loch Morlich below Cairn Gorm, he began to serve as a voluntary leader of children's courses in hill-walking. His accord with the young and his passion for instilling safe practice made him an ideal instructor. His appearances at Glenmore Lodge, at first infrequent, so greatly increased when the centre moved uphill to its present site, that he sold his Arrochar house in 1970 and moved to Aviemore, where he lived till he died seven years later. When he became unable to lead groups to the hills, he turned his botanical skills to the creation of a heather and alpine rockery at the front of the Lodge. It is still there today, one of several memorials to his energetic loves. Another is this book, for he loved the Cuillin more than any other mountains. To them he offered his best work, declaring on its first page, 'They have no equal in all the world.' He said it again when he gave me a copy of the book. I knew from his voice that he meant it.

W.H. MURRAY © 1986

The Cuillin and their names

THE Cuillin are a comparatively small range of mountains tucked away in a corner of the Isle of Skye, the main group—the Black Cuillin—occupying an area of about thirty square miles. They are the most notable mountains in Britain and have no equal in all the world.

The main range could be described as in the shape of a rough horseshoe with one heel short. Making up this horseshoe of about eight miles are twenty-three peaks, most of them about three thousand feet high, and all connected by ridges which never fall below two thousand five hundred feet. From the outer side of the horseshoe several spurs project towards Glen Brittle, enclosing between them the characteristic Cuillin corries. Streams drain from each of these corries, and some of the streams have their source in lochans high up among the mountains. On the inner side of the horseshoe one spur carries the peaks of the Dubhs, while another longer one runs south-easterly from about the mid-point of the range, enclosing between it and the main range the far-famed valley of Coruisk.

Standing apart from the main range but of the same geological structure is the separate mountain of Blaven. Grouped around Sligachan are a lesser range of hills known as the Red Cuillin whose reddish granite contrasts with the black gabbro of their neighbours and which offer no scope for the rock climber.

Strong walkers may gain the summits of all our mainland hills. To only a few of the Cuillin peaks are there easy ways and even those involve a fair amount of scrambling, while a good many of the peaks are for rock climbers only. For the rock climber the supreme thing is the gabbro rock, a rough,

I

hard, crystalline structure with a profusion of holds and which is not met with elsewhere in Britain other than in the adjoining Isle of Rhum. So prickly the rock that finger-tips become quite tender after much contact and gloves are often recommended, even for summer climbing. Gabbro is almost adhesive and highly destructive to the integrity of the nether garments. But not all Cuillin rock is tough and sound. This gabbro is a later intrusion in the older basalt which has mostly weathered away. Here and there it remains, smooth, and, when wet, slippery, and does not offer such secure holds as the gabbro.

All kinds of climbing are there for the cragsman's delight—faces, gullies, buttresses, cracks, chimneys—but the true glory of the Cuillin lies in ridge wandering, finding one's way along the narrow shattered ridges, sometimes among the clouds, with the weird towers and pinnacles looming up out of the mist and barring the way; sometimes on the very top of the world, with wondrous Hebrid panoramas all round. I cannot think of the Cuillin as black. Light grey, steel blue, rose-flushed in dawn, tipped blood-red in the evening sun— all these I have seen and many others. Yet it cannot be denied that they are more normally sombre and black, which gave rise to the legend that no vegetation grows among them. There is vegetation, albeit sparse, even on the wind-swept summit ridges, and many flowers grow in the high corries; a complete flora of the Cuillin has not yet been made.

In Scotland there has been too great a worship of mountains over three thousand feet high, some of which are within a thousand feet of a main road, involving only an insignificant climb. The roads around the Cuillin are at sea-level. Every inch must be gained by Shanks's nag, so that the Cuillin look their height; indeed they often look ten thousand feet high. Mist and clouds belong to the Cuillin, adding grandeur and giving height. Much of their magic would vanish did they always stand out stark and clear.

Sombre and black they may be, but what a feast of colour from their summits! What a contrast between the black rocks around and the glittering blues and greens of lochs and seas far below, the lushness of Glen Brittle, sun-kissed waves breaking on golden sands and the softer colouring of mainland hills fading away in the distance! Then at sunset every colour of tartan streaks the heavens and western seas are a race of flowing gold.

Cuillin climbing is very definitely holiday climbing. Some have even preferred a holiday in the Cuillin to a holiday in the Alps. Even a moderate Alpine peak will mean a crowded hut, an early start in darkness and always a sense of urgency to return before the midday sun softens snow slopes and sets loose frost-bound rocks. In the Cuillin, in summer at least, there is no sense of urgency. Darkness is short. One may climb by night as by day, see the magic of dawn and the glory of sunset from the high tops. Add to that the glorious bathing pools in every corrie and the choice of Skye does not seem out of place.

Always there is controversy as to the meaning of the name given to these great peaks. The early writers had considerable difficulty as to Gaelic spelling, a difficulty not unknown to many of us today. The name has appeared as Cuilluelum, Cullaelum, Quillin, Cullin, Cuchullin, Coolin, Coolins, Cuillin, Cuillins. In this book the Ordnance Survey version, Cuillin, is given throughout, except in certain quotations from earlier writers. Nor is there any need to add the word hills. The Cuillin are mountains in their own right, worthy to stand alone like the Alps, the Caucasus and the Himalaya.

We can, according to our inclination and reading, interpret the name as a survival from the heroic age, or from Norse, Welsh or Gaelic.

It is noticeable that the name Cuchullin first appeared after the publication of Macpherson's *Ossian*, in which Cuchullin figures as the great hero of the Gael. Most of us know the Saga by this time—how Cuchullin (or Cuthullin, Cuchulainn or Cuchullan, according to the fancy of his chroniclers) came from Ireland to learn the art of war under the great Queen Sgathach, the Amazon who reigned at Dunskaith Castle in Skye; how he married her daughter and went off to the Irish wars; how his son, in manhood, followed the fighting trail to Ireland and was killed by his father who did not recognise him.

Another story tells how Cuchullin was but one of many sons sent by kings of Ireland to Skye and how, at the end of the first year, a test of their progress was whether they could walk across "the bridge of cliffs" which was described in the legend:

> "Wonderful was the sight the bridge afforded, for it narrowed until it became so narrow as the hair of one's head, the second time it shortened till it became as an inch, and the third time it grew slippery as an eel of the river and the fourth time it rose up high as the mast of a ship."

This was supposed to be a part of the Cuillin, some say the Pinnacle Ridge of Sgurr nan Gillean, and as Cuchullin was the only person ever to perform the feat the mountains were named in his honour.

There are many other stories of Cuchullin and it would be very fitting were such mighty peaks named after such a mighty warrior, but there is no real evidence to support it. The ancients were not in the habit of naming mountains after people (the claim that Ben Lomond is named after a Celtic hero Laomain is not generally accepted). The oldest place-names are the simplest possible description of the place as it was at that time. This explains the many Ben More's in Scotland. The people of old did not travel much, hence the biggest hill in their own vicinity became Ben More. So with many other common names.

One Gaelic interpretation is from A'Chuilionn, meaning "holly", apparently referring to the supposed resemblance of the skyline of the ridge to the edge of a holly leaf. But the holly tree is not very common in Skye and the resemblance is not one which would readily occur to the observer. According to another theory it is because the gabbro rock of the Cuillin is so prickly to the touch. Against that is the fact that the peaks were practically unknown and unclimbed, so that the prickly rock would also be unknown.

That so much weight has been given to the "holly" interpretation is due to the prestige of him who supported it so strongly, Sheriff Nicolson, who was so great an authority on matters relating to Skye.

Colin Phillip also did much research in the matter of place-names in Skye, and mentions that in Wales they have an old Celtic word "Coolin" meaning worthless. Now that the Cuillin provide us with endless delights it seems sacrilege to describe them as worthless, yet so would they appear to the ancients, for these rocky hills provide but little pasturage, though I have seen sheep in the main ridge of the Cuillin and there are relics of summer sheilings in some of the corries.

Professor Forbes in his account of *Norway and its Glaciers* (1851) writes of "the mountains of Northern Norway—commonly called the Kjölen range". The name still appears in school maps used in Norway today, the range in the north between Norway and Sweden being marked Kjölen. According to the dictionary Kjöl means keel (of a boat) and ridge (of mountains), so that the name is simple and appropriate. The name is a very old one and it is very likely that the word Cuillin is derived from it, for the Norsemen were acquainted with Skye from the eighth century, were in actual occupation for hundreds of years and have left us a vast number of place-names all over the north-west of Scotland. The Vikings named many outstanding landmarks especially as seen from the sea and surely they could not have failed to name that great range. Remember also that a lesser peak, Beinn na Caillich, has associations with the Norsemen.

4

The Cuillin and their Names

Considering all these things I suggest that the Cuillin were named in those far-off days and that the association with Cuchullin was wishful thinking of later years. This would rule out Sheriff Nicolson's interpretation, as he took it to be modern Gaelic, and also the Welsh one, as that country had little association with Skye.

Though all connected by ridges, the various peaks have a definite individuality of their own and, with the exception of those named after climbers, their names have some connection with their appearance or with the corries below them. Usually there is a viewpoint from where each peak shows to best advantage. From Sligachan, Sgurr nan Gillean appears a most noble mountain of classical outline; Sgurr a' Ghreadaidh is best viewed from the Coruisk side; Sgurr a' Mhadaidh from Coire na Creiche and Sgurr Dubh from Loch Scavaig. Sgurr Mhic Coinnich's best viewpoint is Lochan Coire Lagan, while Sgurr Alasdair, with Sgurr Thearlaich and Sgurr Sgumain as supporting outlines, is impressive from many aspects.

The names and heights here given coincide with the numbering on the line map on page 6:

1. Sgurr na h-Uamha (2,420) – Peak of the Cave
2. Sgurr nan Gillean (3,176) – Peak of Ghylls or Gullies
3. Am Basteir (3,070) – The Executioner
4. Bruach na Frithe (3,143) – Brae of the Forest
5. Sgurr an Fheadain (2,215) – Peak of the Water-pipe
6. Bidein Druim nan Ramh (2,850) – Peak of Ridge of Oars
7. Sgurr a' Mhadaidh (2,935) – The Fox's Peak
8. Sgurr a' Ghreadaidh (3,190) – The Peak of Mighty Winds or The Peak of Clear Waters
9. Sgurr Thormaid (3,090) – Norman's Peak
10. Sgurr na Banachdich (3,167) – The Milkmaid's Peak
11. Sgurr Dearg (3,026) – The Red Peak
12. Inaccessible Pinnacle of Sgurr Dearg
13. Sgurr Mhic Coinnich (3,017) – Mackenzie's Peak
14. Sgurr Thearlaich (3,201) – Peak of Charles
15. Sgurr Alasdair (3,251) – Peak of Alexander
16. Sgurr Sgumain (3,104) – The Stack Peak
17. Sgurr Dubh na Da Bheinn (3,064) – The Black Peak of the Two Hills
18. Sgurr Dubh Mor (3,084) – The Big Black Peak

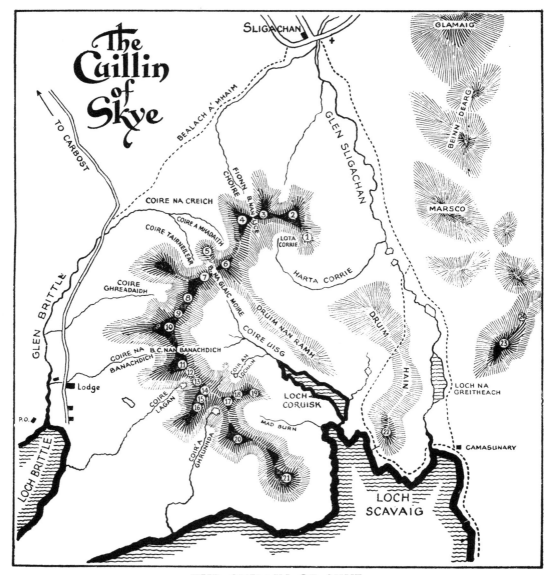

THE CUILLIN OF SKYE

23. Blaven (3,041) – The Hill of Bloom
24. Clach Glas (2,590) – The Grey Stone

The chief corries are:

Coir' a' Bhasteir – between Pinnacle Ridge of Sgurr nan Gillean and Sgurr a' Bhasteir.

Fhionn Choire (Fair Corrie) – between Sgurr a' Bhasteir and Bruach na Frithe.

Coire na Creiche (Corrie of the Spoil, commemorating a clan fight between the MacLeods and the MacDonalds), which is divided by Sgurr an Fheadain into Coir' a' Mhadaidh and Coire Tairneilear (the Thunderer). As the latter leads up to Sgurr a' Mhadaidh the supposition is that the Ordnance Survey named these two corries in wrong order.

Coir' a' Ghreadaidh – leads up to the peak of that name and is bounded by Sgurr Thuilm and Sgurr na Gobhar, both of which are on spurs running westwards.

Coire na Banachdich – between Sgurr na Gobhar and Sgurr na Banachdich and leads up to the bealach.

Coire Lagan (Corrie of the Hollow) – bounded by Sgurr Dearg and its westwards ridge, Sgurr Mhic Coinnich, Sgurr Thearlaich, Sgurr Alasdair and Sgurr Sgumain.

Coir' a' Ghrunnda (the Floor Corrie) – surrounded by Sgurr Sgumain, Sgurr Alasdair and Sgurr Dubh.

An Garbh-choire (Rough Corrie) – between the Dubhs and the south end of main ridge; the Mad Burn flows from this corrie.

Coir' an Lochain – between the Dubhs and Sgurr Coir' an Lochain.

Coireachan Rudha (Red Corries) – As the name implies it has two branches leading up to Bealach Coire Lagan and Bealach Coire na Banachdich respectively. It is surrounded by the peaks from Sgurr Coir' an Lochain to Sgurr a' Ghreadaidh.

Harta Corrie – leads westwards from Glen Sligachan towards the ridge and is named Lota Corrie (Loft Corrie) in its upper part.

The chief passes across the main ridge are:

Bealach nan Lice – leads from Fhionn Choire to Lota Corrie
Bealach na Glaic Moire – leads from Coire na Creiche to Coruisk
Bealach Coire na Banachdich – leads from Glen Brittle to Coruisk

The Past

THE EARLY TRAVELLERS

WHO first climbed a Skye mountain? Of the greater peaks our information is fairly accurate, though unknown shepherds probably crossed the high passes and gained some of the peaks prior to the climbers who have the honour.

Apart from the Cuillin, Beinn na Caillich must have known climbers since the earliest of times. The evidence is there for all to see—that huge circular cairn on its summit contrasting with the few stones which mark other Skye peaks and far larger than any cairn on our mainland mountains. So we go back to the eighth century and the legend of the Norse princess who lived and died at Castle Maoil at Kyleakin and who was buried on the black windswept summit of Beinn an Caillich, her followers erecting the cairn over her bier. If the story be not true why the great cairn and why the name, which means "Mount of the Old Woman"? Expeditions have gone to explore the tombs of the Pharaohs: might not archaeologists dig below Beinn na Caillich's cairn and let us know if it ever was a burial-place? But perhaps we should be content with the legend.

The earliest description of Skye from personal observation was by Dean Munro in 1549: "The iyle is callit by the Erishe, Ellan Skyane, that is to say in English, the Wingitt ile, be reason it has maney wyngs and points lyand furth frae it through the devyding of thir lochs."

He also introduces us to the Cuillin: "In this ile . . . maney woods, maney forrests, maney deire, fair hunting game, maney grate hills principally Cuilluelm and Glannock" (Cuillin and Glamaig).

The first name appeared on a map in 1654, when Timothy Pont produced

8

"The Yle of Skye" and named therein "Culluelun, or Guillin hills". This map was very inaccurate, missing out the whole peninsula of Sleat, yet it was the basis for all such maps for a hundred years.

The first description of Skye written by a native of the island appears in Martin Martin's *Description of the Western Islands of Scotland* in 1703. The mountain names read strangely to us, for he calls them "Quillin, Scornifiey, Bein-store, Bein-vore-scowe, Bein-chro, Bein-nin-Kaillaich". Of these one can only identify Cuillin, The Storr, Marsco and Beinn na Caillich. One doubts his powers of observation when he states that "some of them are covered with snow on the top in summer", but is inclined to agree with: "The Quillin is said to be the cause of much rain, by breaking the clouds which hover about it, which quickly after pour down in rain upon the quarter on which the wind then blows."

The book's chief interest lies in the fact that Samuel Johnson read it when he was a young man and it is very probable that it induced him to make his famous trip to the Hebrides in his later years. Indeed a copy of the first edition now in the National Library in Edinburgh bears the inscription in Boswell's handwriting: "This very book accompanied Mr Samuel Johnson and me on our tour of the Hebrides in 1773."

Strangely, however, the first visitor of whom we have any account of actually forsaking known routes and travelling over the Skye mountains was a Prince of the Realm, none other than Prince Charles Edward Stuart. One would like to add that he climbed the hills for pleasure; alas, he only looked upon them as a hiding-place when he was a fugitive. Yet we must honour him even though his journey was among the lesser Red Cuillin rather than among the greater Black Cuillin. Records only tell us that he journeyed by night over the hills from Portree to Elgol, and that at one place he was bogged almost to the waist. His actual route can only be conjectured, but most likely it would be from Portree southwards towards Sligachan. Soldiers were stationed there, hence there would be a detour inland over a very boggy area, crossing the Red Burn, the moor above the present inn and the River Sligachan further up the glen. The obvious route would be to continue up Glen Sligachan, traverse Strath na Creitheach to Camasunary and continue round the coast to Elgol. But the Prince in his wanderings in 1746 seldom took the obvious route and there are strong local legends associating Strath Mor with him. If he travelled via that strath then he would go over the col between Marsco and Beinn Dearg, descend to the head of Loch Ainort and circle round Glas

9

Bheinn Mhor into Strath Mor, thence to Loch Slapin and in the direction of the present road from Torran to Elgol.

Let anyone who doubts Prince Charlie's powers as a hillman follow that route over the hills through the night.

Next came one who gave us the first account of an actual mountain climb in Skye (1772). Thomas Pennant was a Welsh squire whose perfect landscape was a fertile populated valley and who was rather bewildered by the mountains of Scotland. They surprised him. The desolation and the unknown also rather frightened him, yet sometimes we get the beginning of appreciation of mountain grandeur. He reaches the summit of Beinn na Caillich:

"... The prospect to the west was of desolation itself; a savage series of rude mountains, discoloured, black and red, as if by the rage of fire ... the serrated tops of Blaven affect with astonishment and beyond them the clustered height of Quillin, or the mountains of Cuchullin, like its hero stood like a hill that catches the clouds of heaven."

A year later brought Samuel Johnson and James Boswell on their famous journey. Though they were a month in Skye, Johnson never once mentions the Cuillin. To us today it seems incredible that he should have stayed at Talisker and passed by Carbost and Sligachan without the greatest range of rock peaks in Britain making the slightest impression on him. To Johnson mountains were merely inconveniences: "A walk upon ploughed fields in England is a dance upon carpets compared to the toilsome drudgery of wandering in Skye." The only mountain he mentions is Beinn na Caillich, perhaps because of the legend attached to it: "The hill behind the house we did not climb ... to climb steeps is very laborious and to descend them dangerous"—scarcely the mood of the mountaineer.

There might be some excuse for Johnson, for he was sixty-four at that time and probably his eyesight was bad. During the day he was fully preoccupied with the difficulties of the journey, riding over rough country where roads were non-existent. So much so that he scarcely noticed the scenery, while at night he entered into his own kingdom—good talk round a good fire.

There could be no excuse for Boswell, who was then a young and active man. He, at least, did see the Cuillin—"a prodigious range of mountains, capped with rocky pinnacles in a strange variety of shapes". That was all. As with Pennant the mountains merely "affected with astonishment". Boswell tells how he climbed Dun Caan in Raasay (1,351 feet) and says that the locals

10

claimed it to be higher than the peaks of Skye. He makes no effort to dispute the statement, though he must have seen, just a few miles away, the magnificent range of the Cuillin, twice as high as Dun Caan. Like most early travellers he seemed unable to estimate heights.

The next traveller we hear of is Robert Jameson in 1800. He followed Pennant's footsteps up Beinn na Caillich; to him also the Cuillin were "dark lurid and terrible summits".

Dr John MacCulloch toured the Highlands extensively from 1811 to 1821 and wrote voluminously. While Pennant admired only the gentle pastoral views, MacCulloch could appreciate every aspect of the mountain scene:

> " . . . It towers aloft in simple sublimity; it is the singular felicity of this mountain, that, while its outline is everywhere elegant and graceful, its simplicity and breadth of form serve to support and to harmonise according to the true rule of beauty, whether in nature or in art, that endless variety of parts of which it consists."

True, it was not for their aesthetic value that he sought out mountains: it was geology that urged him to "risk his neck every day on mountain and precipice and his whole carcass in flood and in ford". After all, mountaineering owes much to the scientists, who were, in fact, the first mountaineers in Scotland as elsewhere. Very many years were to elapse before people could appreciate that there was pleasure in ascending a mountain, not with any scientific object in view, but merely for the sake of the mountain.

MacCulloch's ambition to construct a geological map of Scotland, "with all its bright arrays of blues and greys and greens and browns", took him up Ben Lomond, The Cobbler, Ben Ledi, Ben Venue, Schiehallion, Cruachan, Goatfell, Ben Lawers, Cairngorm, An Teallach and many other peaks. His methods were scarcely those of a climber of today, for he considered that a mountain had special merit if he could ride all the way to its summit. Now and then the true spirit of the mountaineer shines through. Of course he went to Skye and like his predecessors climbed Beinn na Caillich: "Being there you wish to be on Ben something else, and then a stage higher, and so on till you come to the Cuchullin Hills, just as in the climbs we make in this world, political and philosophical."

The Cuillin are not for one who prefers to make an ascent on horseback. All his efforts were unsuccessful, though he tried seven times in five successive seasons. One must doubt his statement that it was merely weather conditions which foiled him every time. Was it not perhaps his experience when he found himself stuck on a rock face unable to ascend or descend? There he passed "the longest five minutes of his life" before he managed to extricate himself.

The truth would seem to be that MacCulloch was the first to discover that climbing on the mainland of Scotland and climbing among the Cuillin were quite different propositions, that in spite of the many peaks he had ascended, the Cuillin were beyond his powers. To excuse himself he sums up by describing the upper peaks as mere rocks, with acclivities so steep and smooth as to render all access impossible. It was he who first mentioned Loch Coruisk:

> "I found the place which, excepting the shepherd of Strathaird, mortal foot had scarce trod. . . . So suddenly and unexpectedly does the strange scene break upon the view, so unlike is it to the sea-bay without, so dissimilar to all other scenery, and so little to be foreseen in a narrow isolated spot like Skye that I felt as if transported by some magician into the enchanted wilds of an Arabian tale, carried to the habitations of Genii among the recesses of the Caucasus. Here the sun never shone since creation, and a thousand reflected lights, mingling with the aerial tints, gave a singular solemnity to the huge irregular masses which now rose overhead, deeply cleft by the torrents that were now at length audibly foaming down the black precipices and which gradually diminishing till they were lost in the misty mountain summit, seemed to have their sources in the invisible region of the clouds."

MacCulloch walked round Loch Coruisk with his guides, and, towards evening, climbed some way up Sgurr na Stri alone. None of the four men would accompany him, all being somewhat scared. "Ech," said one, "this is an awfu-like place."

It is strange that MacCulloch should have given such a fanciful description when his accounts of views from mainland hills are mostly trustworthy. It must have been the unknown and the wish to make the peaks which had defeated him the more awful. It is significant that he gives no details whatever of his repeated attempts to scale them.

MacCulloch's fanciful description of Coruisk has lingered on even till today. In a magazine article a well-known writer gave, as one of the wonders of Scotland, Loch Coruisk—the loch on which the sun never shines. A glance at a map and a moment's thought would have shown him his error. Coruisk is two miles long and almost half a mile broad. Were the sun never to touch it

1. Loch Coruisk

2. The Cuillin from Elgol

3. Of the early paintings of Loch Coruisk, George Fennel Robson's (above) is by far the most accurate, while Turner's impression (No. 4) has no resemblance to actuality. Nor will many agree with Ruskin's dictum that it is "the perfect impression of inferior mountains". All early sketches tend to magnify the peaks and make their summits much sharper and steeper, as in the sketch of Sligachan and Sgurr nan Gillean about 1860, by an unknown artist, (No. 5)

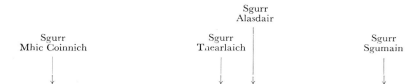

Sgurr
Mhic Coinnich

Sgurr
Alasdair

Sgurr
Thearlaich

Sgurr
Sgumain

10. The Sgurr Alasdair massif from the ridge leading from Glen Brittle to Sgurr Dearg. From here Alexander Nicolson descended into upper Coire Lagan and then made the first ascent of Sgurr Alasdair by way of the Great Stone Shoot in 1873. The first ascent of Sgurr Mhic Coinnich in 1887 was by way of the ridge on the left while the first ascent of Sgurr Thearlaich was direct from Coire Lagan, starting from about the same place as Nicolson and then bearing to the left over the rocks.

– – – – Route of Nicolson's first ascent, 1873
× × × × Route of Collie's face climb, 1896
· – · – · – Route of Abraham's face climb, 1907

11. Sheriff Nicolson

12. Blaven and Clach Glas from Loch Slapin. The first recorded ascent was by Professor Nicol and
Algernon Swinbourne in 1857, but they gave no particulars of their exact route. The easiest route is
indicated and is probably the route taken by them

it would have to be much narrower and the mountains would have to rise up perpendicularly from its banks like a New York skyscraper.

The garrulous MacCulloch had not much of a public. We may take it that Loch Coruisk was still generally unknown till Sir Walter Scott told us of it. In 1814 he sailed to the Hebrides in the Lighthouse Commissioner's ship, landed by rowing-boat at Loch Scavaig and walked up to Coruisk. Everyone knows his immortal description in *The Lord of the Isles*:

> *For rarely human eye has known*
> *A scene so stern as that dread lake*
> *With its dark ledge of barren stone.*
>
> *. . . above—around—below*
> *Nor tree, nor shrub, nor plant, nor flower*
> *Nor aught of vegetative power*
> *The weary eye may ken.*

To the poet, poetic licence, but we would expect much more accuracy in the diary of so acute an observer as the Wizard of the North. Yet, while not so fanciful as MacCulloch, it is not much more accurate.

> "They (the Cuillin) seemed to consist of precipitous sheets of naked rock, down which torrents were leaping in a hundred lines of foam. The tops, apparently inaccessible to human foot, were rent and split into the most tremendous pinnacles."

So far so good, but with Coruisk he fails.

> "Vegetation there was little or none, and the mountains rose so perpendicularly from the water's edge that Borrowdale is a jest to them. . . . We penetrated so far as distinctly to observe the termination of the lake under an immense mountain which rises absolutely from the head of the waters. . . . The opposite side of the lake seemed quite pathless, as a huge mountain sinks in a profound and almost perpendicular precipice down to the water. I never saw a spot on which there was less appearance of vegetation of any kind; the eye rested on nothing but broken and naked crags, and the rocks on which we walked by the side of the loch were as bare as the pavement of Cheapside."

Obviously Sir Walter only went a little way up the lochside or he would have seen the pleasant oasis of greenery at its far end; seen, too, that far from the mountains rising absolutely from the end of the loch, they are fully two miles distant.

The sheer magnificence of the scene must have prevented him from taking in the smaller details. Certainly to the casual glance from a distance there is little appearance of vegetation, but as one walks by the lochside one may discover it in abundance—heather, ferns, bracken, brambles and many wild flowers.

Just as the publication of *The Lady of the Lake* started the tourist trek to the Trossachs, so did the appearance of *The Lord of the Isles* set the tourists on their way to Skye, with Coruisk as their main objective. Guide-book writers came on the scene and Coruisk was mentioned in Anderson's Guide-book of 1836. Many came, visited Loch Coruisk from Loch Scavaig, and departed. None left the beaten track. None sought the mountain-tops.

G. F. Robson, a London artist, was one of the first to attempt to put Loch Coruisk and the Cuillin on to canvas. He was a very faithful delineator of the mountain scene and gained fame with his series of etchings of the Grampians. His water-colour of Coruisk (now in South Kensington Museum) is a worthy attempt to reproduce the scenery of the wildest of our Scottish lochs, though, alas, in keeping with artists of his time, he had to insert a kilted figure in the foreground. (No. 3.)

William Danielson travelled extensively in Scotland about this period, and his sketches, which were published in 1819, gained wide popularity. Included among them are views of the Cuillin from Raasay, from Sligachan and from Loch Scavaig, all making the mountains much higher and more pointed. Reproductions of these prints now adorn the walls of the lounge at Sligachan Hotel and it is not surprising that peaks so depicted by the artist daunted the early travellers.

Not so happy was Turner's "Loch Coriskin". This was in 1831 when he was commissioned to make twenty-four drawings to illustrate Scott's poetical works. J. M. W. Turner was then at the zenith of his fame. But Turner, from the time of his first mountain painting—the famous "Kilchurn"—had, as a later critic so justly put it, "already abandoned everything in the nature of topographic fidelity".

Ruskin in his *Modern Painters* describes Turner's "Coriskin" as "the perfect impression of the Inferior Mountains". Thus did he slander the Cuillin. No "Inferior Mountains" these, but mountains which can hold their own with any mountain groups throughout the world. To Ruskin everything which

Turner drew was perfect and *Modern Painters* might almost be described as a eulogy of Turner. Looking at that drawing, can anyone really say "he drew the precipices and the gloomy lake with great fidelity to the character of the place"? Not so—no one could ever trace the faintest resemblance to Sgurr Dubh. It is more as if the place had been revealed to him suddenly in a dream and he had attempted to draw it when he woke up. Undoubtedly Turner was tremendously impressed by the scene and himself tells us how he proved Sir Walter's "no vegetation" description to be wrong, as he slipped when searching for a stance, and would have broken his neck but for some turf which he was able to grasp. (No. 4.)

The route to Loch Coruisk from the north via Glen Sligachan and over the Drum Hain ridge became known and was often used by foresters and shepherds.

The Rev. C. Lesingham Smith (1835) gives us the first description of Sligachan Inn. It must have been a small place, but even in those far-off days the feeding was grand.

Smith tells us of a sober meal of stewed meat, kipper-salmon and oatcakes and an extensive breakfast with countless mutton chops and eggs. He needed that breakfast, for he was setting out on the first adventurous trip among the Cuillin. He had already endeavoured to reach Loch Coruisk by sea from Elgol, but had been driven back by stormy weather, so determined to reach it by land.

Smith, as always in his journeys, carried his trusty umbrella, and the sturdy forester who was his guide carried a goodly supply of victuals and whisky. Four hours was the usual time for the walk to Coruisk. Smith did it in two and a half hours in spite of diverging to have a look at Harta Corrie and sheltering from rain under the Bloody Stone. His description of Coruisk is more accurate than that of previous travellers, perhaps because he saw it under a bright sun and a blue sky.

The forester who had taken many other visitors to Coruisk was much impressed by Smith's strong walking, and suggested they should try and return by a different route direct over the ridge at the head of Loch Coruisk and into Lota Corrie (the upper section of Harta Corrie). The forester himself had never ventured there, but had seen deer climbing up and thought that where deer had gone he could follow. This ridge is a subsidiary Cuillin ridge, rising to a height of fifteen hundred feet, and the route over it is not too easy, as there are huge glaciated slabs on the Coruisk side.

To the forester's proposal Smith replied, "This is a very weighty proposition, for to scale these rocks is no trifle, so if you please we'll sit down by this brook and take our dinner first and then hold a council of war." Then, after having attacked the mutton-ham and biscuits, and made a considerable vacuum in the whisky flask, he declared himself ready for the climb.

At first all went well, but when they had to crawl on hands and knees Smith found his umbrella a sad nuisance. At steeper parts he pushed up the forester, who pulled him up in turn. So it went on by clefts, rocks and chimneys, now and then beating a retreat and "angling round". "A single false step would have hurled us to destruction and there was very great danger that the first man would loosen some stone that might sweep down the hindmost." At last a smooth and perpendicular rock barred their way; once more they turned back, "angled round", surmounted every obstacle and "stepped forth proudly and joyously upon the very topmost crag".

"You are the first gentleman," said the forester, "that ever made the pass; nothing but a shepherd or a red deer has ever been before us." Smith was well rewarded, for the tops were clear. The "infernal chasm" of Coruisk lay far below; beyond it the bays of Camasunary and Scavaig, sparkling Atlantic seas with the isles of Eigg and Rhum and others of the Hebrides.

They found an easy way down to Harta Corrie and trekked through Glen Sligachan by the way they had come. They had taken seven hours for the whole journey, and the landlady, not expecting them till much later, had not dinner ready for them.

Such was the first climber among the Cuillin who faced the unknown and won through.

THE SCIENTIST

Lesingham Smith's pass-storming was a fitting prelude to the ascent of the great peaks. Mountains such as these deserved a conqueror worthy of them. So was it. None more worthy than the great scientist Professor James Forbes —the wonder child of his generation—who became Professor of Natural Philosophy at the University of Glasgow when only twenty-three years of age. As with early climbers elsewhere, it was the pursuit of science which took him to the mountains. As a boy of seventeen he had visited Chamonix and had been enthralled by the glaciers and the story of de Saussure's experiments among them. Thus it was that the Alps were the scene of his greatest work, for he was a physicist first, a geologist only second and the Alps were a laboratory to him.

After he was appointed to a professorship at Edinburgh, every long summer vacation for nigh on twenty years was spent among the mountains. His first was in England, his second in the Pyrenees, his third in Skye. He was then twenty-seven years of age and described by a friend as having "a dignified and commanding presence and gentle and refined manners, wielded by a will of rare strength, purity and elevation". The fact that the high Cuillin were deemed inaccessible did not deter him; he decided at once to climb Sgurr nan Gillean.

He engaged Lord MacDonald's forester, Duncan MacIntyre, the same man who had guided Lesingham Smith. Just as the forester recognised Smith as apart from the usual run of tourists, so did he see the climber in Forbes, and revealed to him that, though he himself had tried Sgurr nan Gillean several times, he thought he could find another route which had not previously been tried and which would lead to the summit. So it proved. MacIntyre must have had a true eye for the mountains, for on July 7th, 1836, he led Forbes up by that route now known as the tourist route, and gained the summit without much difficulty. Forbes at once noticed what has appealed to countless mountaineers since then, how the extra roughness of the rocks makes them ideally suitable for climbing, and so renders the ascent safe, where with any other formation it might be dangerous. He built a cairn and put up a flag which he states remained for a whole year, but no flag could withstand Cuillin storms for a year. (No. 9.)

For years after that he travelled extensively in the Alps, his great work being the study of the glaciers, all this being recorded in his famous book *Travels in the Alps* which was published in 1843.

When he returned to Skye in 1845, he observed the Cuillin more closely, and his practised eye noticed the result of glacial action. Again with Duncan MacIntyre he made the first ascent of Bruach na Frithe. This time he carried a barometer, and, after taking readings on the summit, proposed to MacIntyre to try to ascend Sgurr nan Gillean from there and note the difference in heights between the peaks. Forbes always took the easiest route and gave no thought of trying to keep to the narrow ridge by way of Am Basteir. He deemed that utterly impossible, so made a long descent into Lota Corrie, and then had a stiff scramble up Sgurr nan Gillean, a much steeper route than that of 1836. His readings made the height of Sgurr nan Gillean 3,200 feet, and that of Bruach na Frithe about forty feet lower. (O.S. heights now give 3,167 and 3,143 feet respectively.)

Forbes must have crossed the range by several of the passes, for the map which he drew was far in advance of anything which had previously appeared. It was, in fact, the first map which showed the Cuillin with any resemblance of accuracy. Arrowsmith's original map of 1807 did not even show Loch Coruisk. Of course MacCulloch inserted Coruisk, his being the first map to show it; as he did not gain the peaks the only one he mentions is Sgurr na Stri.

Forbes described his map as an "eye sketch", but it is a very good general plan of the main ridge and some of its branches. The peaks which are here for the first time named and placed with rough accuracy are Sgurr nan Gillean, Bruach na Frithe, Sgurr na Banachdich and Gars-bheinn, Sgurr na Stri is here called Trodhu and the name Strona Stri given to Druim nam Ramh.

The result of Forbes's travels in Skye was his paper "On the Geology of the Cuchullin Hills", which was published in the *Edinburgh Philosophical Journal*. At the end of that paper is a most interesting article "On the traces of ancient glaciers in the Cuchullin Hills", in which he writes:

"Having hitherto taken no share in the discussions raised as to the proof of glacial action in this country, and being as much indisposed as ever to embark on a theory which offers such evident difficulties, I yet feel it to be a duty to make known what I have observed in connection with it among the Cuchullin Hills, phenomena so singular and well marked as to require a steady and patient consideration in whatever way they may be attempted to be explained and which I am compelled to admit must now be unhesitatingly ascribed to the action of moving ice, rather than to any other kind of agency with which we are acquainted."

Though Forbes showed the way to the high tops, others were slow to follow and still contented themselves with Loch Coruisk. Still we read of the "grisly mountains" that "seemed to rise and menace us looking so dark and surly" (John Wilson in 1841), though Lord Cockburn, in the same year, proved himself a much more accurate observer, as befitted a judge. He derides the idea of perpendicular mountains of wall-like appearance and is very critical of Scott not allowing any vegetable life, himself noting a dozen of the ordinary wild-flowers. Yet still there is a feeling of awe: " . . . No mind can resist this impression. Every prospect and every object is excluded, except which are held within that short and narrow valley; and within that there is nothing

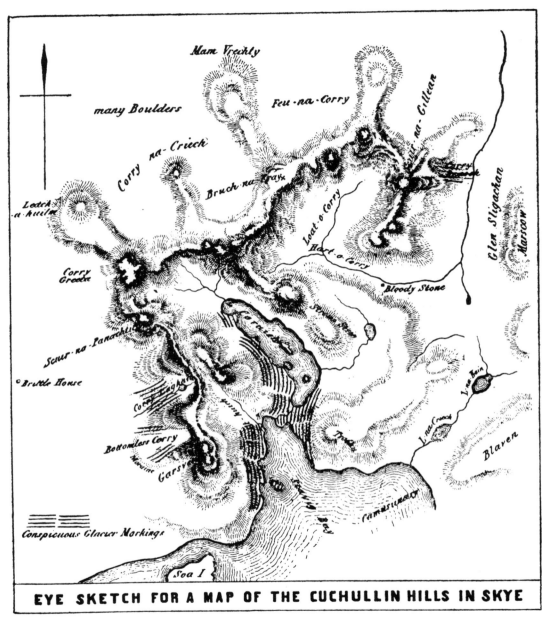

EYE SKETCH FOR A MAP OF THE CUCHULLIN HILLS IN SKYE

PROFESSOR FORBES'S EYE SKETCH OF THE CUILLIN

except the little loch, towered over by the high and grisly forms of these storm-defying and man-despising mountains." Scarcely the mood for the mountaineer but man-defying the Cuillin certainly were after Professor Forbes had departed from the scene.

The Rev. Thomas Grierson also visited Skye in 1841. Like MacCulloch he claimed the ascent of many a mainland mountain from the Merrick to Ben More Assynt, including five times up Schiehallion. Some of his descriptions, however, make us doubt his accuracy. He was accustomed to do fifteen miles before a nine o'clock breakfast, and tells how he left Ledard on Loch Ard one morning, crossed the mountains to Loch Katrine, where he was boated over by a shepherd; over the mountains *again*, through the Forest of Glen Finglas and its deep and dreary bogs to Balquidder; over the mountains *again* to Glen Dochart and Killin; over the mountains *again* to Glen Lyon; and once more across the mountains to Rannoch-side, which he reached before midnight. As the crow flies the distance is about forty miles; on foot it would be between sixty and seventy miles. Let some of our peak-baggers follow the route described and let us know if it actually can be done in one day.

Nevertheless Grierson was a mighty hill walker and one would have expected great deeds in Skye. He only managed to follow Lesingham Smith's round to Coruisk and back over the ridge, though he did, with a wealth of qualifying adjectives, forecast the ascent of all the great peaks: "I have the best authority (the ministers of Strathaird and Portree) for asserting that an active, cautious, persevering pedestrian may, without immense danger, reach all the highest peaks." Why, after all his boasting, did he not try himself?

In *Household Words* for 1852 an article about Skye appears, presumably written by Charles Dickens, in which he describes the island as "a hilly rocky, misty sort of place with pasture ground and potato fields" and makes no mention whatever of the Cuillin.

When C. S. Inglis's party arrived at Sligachan in 1857, they sought for a guide to take them up Sgurr nan Gillean, but no one could be found who knew the way or who had ever been to the top. Theirs would appear to have been the first guideless ascent and their route was quite different and very much longer than that taken by Professor Forbes. The Glen Sligachan path was followed for five miles, then they turned up Harta Corrie and higher into Lota Corrie, from where the ridge was gained between Sgurr Beag and Sgurr nan Gillean near the point where the usual tourist route reaches it from the other side. From there the summit towered up "like the spire of a cathedral. There seemed scarcely a part for even a bird to rest the sole of her foot upon. It was like climbing the Scott monument on the outside."

Nothing daunted they kept on using hands, knees and feet, "squeezing through singular gaps in the rocks", then "creeping along sharp ledglings", and drawing themselves up a narrow slit in the rock, till at last they gained the summit, when they gave a hearty cheer and proceeded to admire the view. Mist threatening to come down, they beat a retreat and descended by Professor Forbes's route.

It was a very fine effort and it is a pity this resolute party did not attempt further conquests. Others were afoot in Skye that year, and Professor John Nicol of Glasgow and the poet, Algernon Swinburne, climbed Blaven. Nicol merely remarks that they climbed it from Loch Slapin "with no great danger". Blaven is not a difficult climb from this side, and though Nicol and Swinburne did not claim a first ascent, there is no record of anyone having gained the summit of Blaven before them. The ascent seems to have been forgotten, as guide-books of today credit the brothers Willink with the first ascent of Blaven in 1873. (No. 12.)

The Alpine Club was formed in 1857 for "the promotion of good fellowship among mountaineers, of mountain climbing and exploration throughout the world, and of better knowledge of the mountains through literature, science and art", but with so many virgin peaks in the Alps, the club did not, in its early years, give much thought to our homeland hills. When one of its members reached Skye in 1859 he did not put up much of a show. C. R. Weld was doing a grand tour of Scotland and came to Skye to see the "lions"—Coruisk and the Cuillin. Lesingham Smith, that happy wanderer, enjoyed Sligachan even in bad weather, but what can we think of the self-termed mountaineer who writes: " . . . In the midst of barren moorland, treeless, and with nothing to break the sterile prospect but a bridge backed by Ben Glamaig, which was surrounded in mist, it requires considerable philosophy to support the ennui of four days' residence at Sligachan." That of Sligachan where climbers may have to book a year in advance to be sure of accommodation!

Apparently Weld never even thought of following the footsteps of Forbes. His route to Coruisk was "through a grim gorge" to Camasunary, where there was at that time an establishment for reclaiming drunkards. He then hired a boat with four men and was rowed round to Loch Scavaig, made a circuit of the loch and gave us a description in much the usual terms. A day or two later he walked up Glen Sligachan again and climbed Sgurr na Stri from the highest point of the Drum Hain path. There is no difficulty in ascending to the summit from this point, but according to Weld it was six hundred feet of precipitous scaling, frequently up nearly vertical rocks, while on the summit "one leg dangles over Loch Coruisk and the other over the Bay of Camasunary".

And what did he see?

> "Peaks and pinnacles, jagged crests and fantastic outlines; a wilderness of weird shapes, dark, solemn and awful. . . .
>
> "Conceive these mountains if you can—rib them with gleaming waterfalls, paint them with ever changing hues and fill the intervening spaces with gorges, ravines and glens, dashed with purple gloom and abysses filled with steaming mists, and you have some idea of the wondrous Cuillin. Sunshine occasionally illumines their rugged crests, but the darkness of eternal night dwells in their gorges."

There we have it again—the repetition of MacCulloch's statement that "here the sun never shone since creation".

He goes on:

> "Giant Sgurr nan Gillean is there, the monarch of the Cuillin and hear it, brother members of the Alpine Club, another peak a little to the south and inaccessible. At a recent meeting of the club the president drew the attention of members to certain peaks of Continental mountains deemed inaccessible, but here, according to the Admiralty surveyor, is one in the British Isles never trodden by the foot of man. Surely some bold member of the club will scale this Skye peak ere long and tell us that it is but a stroll before breakfast."

It seems incredible that no one took up Weld's challenge; it was actually twenty-one years later before the Inaccessible Pinnacle was first ascended. Imagination boggles at what would happen were an unclimbed peak to be discovered in Scotland today. At once climbers by the dozen would set off for its base and within twenty-one *hours* it would be climbed.

The mapping which Weld mentions was the first attempt to do so by modern methods. As it was an Admiralty effort, the accurate mapping of the coastline was the main objective, Loch Coruisk being shown correctly for the first time. Only a few of the Cuillin peaks are mentioned, the heights being taken by triangulation, those named being Sgurr Dubh, Sgurr Dubh na Da Bheinn, Sgurr Dearg and the Inaccessible, and Sgurr na Gobhar.

Weld met Captain Wood, the surveyor, who told him how he had frequently to wait for weeks to obtain glimpses of the mountain peaks to make his triangulation and how his surveying ship had often been blown into places of great peril.

It was time for a book entirely about Skye and it duly appeared in 1865. Alexander Smith's *A Summer in Skye* was the result of three summer holidays spent with the MacIans at their farm at Ord in Sleat. From there he roamed the moors with "Lachlan Roy" and "Angus-with-the-dogs", gave us that grand description of Broadford Fair and the immortal poem "Blaven":

> *O Blaven, rocky Blaven,*
> *How I long to be with you again,*
> *To see lashed gulf and gully.*
> *Smoke white in the windy rain—*
> *To see in the scarlet sunrise*
> *The mist-wreaths perish with heat,*
> *The wet rock slide with a trickling gleam*
> *Right down to the cataract's feet.*

All who know the Skye mountains will appreciate the description "windy rain"—will have gloried in it, and often have cursed it. Smith was no mountaineer and was content to worship the peaks from afar. Of all the early books about Skye, his alone survives, has gone through many editions and reads as freshly today as when it was written.

THE GREAT EXPLORER

Professor Forbes's accounts of climbing in Skye were confined to scientific journals, while Weld's clarion call reached but a select few. Fittingly it was a man of Skye who brought the Cuillin to wider notice. Alexander Nicolson was born at Husabost in Skye in 1827. In his youth he probably heard about Forbes's climbs, but though he looked upon the Cuillin "with unspeakable awe and admiration" he did not venture among them till he reached manhood. Yet the thought of them must have been with him all during his student days in Edinburgh: "The great blue mass of the Cuillin with profile so clean cut and memorable as a historical face was photographed in my mind before the days of Daguerre and Talbot, and the picture grows not dimmer but more distinct each year."

His aim was, at first, the Ministry of the Free Church of Scotland. In Greek, Latin and Philosophy he was well grounded and was a brilliant Gaelic scholar. Literature fascinated him, and after taking his degree, he made that his career. He was a sub-editor of the eighth edition of *Encyclopædia Britannica,* was on the staff of the short-lived *Edinburgh Guardian* and for a year edited an advanced Liberal paper, the *Daily Express,* till it merged with the *Caledonian Mercury.* He then took up Law and was called to the Scottish Bar in 1860. As an advocate he did not impress, though it has been said he never really had a chance, not having cases offered to him. He eked out a meagre livelihood by law reporting, lecturing and writing, till he was appointed Sheriff-substitute of Kircudbright in 1872. Transferred to Greenock in 1885, he returned to Edinburgh in 1889, where he died in 1893.

He was perhaps the most popular man of his time in Edinburgh, "a big-boned Celt, with a look of strength and kindliness in his large and strongly marked features". With a wonderful charm of manner, a jovial wit and a happy faculty of producing spontaneous rhyme to grace the occasion; he was also a singer and had a real feeling for Gaelic poetry and song. Law was not really his forte; it might have been better had he accepted the Celtic Chair at Edinburgh University, which he was offered before he went to Kirkcudbright.

The soul of the man shines through his articles and his poems. He wrote his own epitaph when he said he "would rather be remembered by one good poem than by many superfluous books". So have his songs of Skye been quoted from that day to this, and will be while the Cuillin remain.

He did not really get to know them till he returned to Skye on holiday in 1865. From then he proceeded to make up for lost time. Not in pursuit of Science did he roam them, but for sheer love of their grandeur which held him from his first climb.

"There is life and movement perpetual in the glorious inspiring air, whether it sighs in the zephyrs or roars in the gale; there is life and music, wild but sweet in the voice of the streams that rush down the corries; there is ever-changing life in the play of the clouds that float serenely through the blue sky or hurry frantically across the riven peaks or descend softly like darkness on the bosom of the hills."

24

Nicolson had visited all the Hebrid Isles and his comparisons between them and Skye are interesting:

"Arran – more delightful,
Islay – the fairest of them all,
Mull has beauty and grandeur – more green and woody,
Jura – Queenly in state, but lacks variety,
Tiree – too flat yet many charms,
Barra – rough and rocky,
Lewis – boggy,
Harris – almost like Skye in mountain grandeur,
Staff and Iona – a universal sense of wonder,
Skye – *Queen of them all.*"

For Weld four days at Sligachan were mere ennui; for Nicolson one day at Sligachan was worth two in most other places. The wild stormy weather was too much for Weld: Nicolson enjoyed it in all its moods, even on his first visit, when a thunderstorm greeted him and "among the towering black mass of the Cuillin rolled and seethed a lurid array of lead coloured clouds, grim and threatening".

He had no patience for visitors who, then, as today, try to rush things in Skye:

"Nor let them imagine that they are all ill-used martyrs if they come for three days and the heavens refuse to show one morsel of blue—if they can't afford to wait for a fair blink the more's the pity for themselves. If they are in a hurry, Skye and its clouds (and its inhabitants) are in none, and the Cuillin will unveil their majestic heads, in due time and no sooner.

"To see them is worth a week's waiting—to see the black peaks start out like living creatures, high above the clouds which wildly career up the cleft ridges, now hiding and now revealing their awful faces, or calmly rising, like the spires and towers of a celestial city, out of a snowy sea of mist, which anon breaks into soft downy wreaths, white and graceful as the sea-birds wing that go gliding with ghost-like ease down the walls of precipices into the dark corries below; and then as softly float up again to the battlements above, leaving bare the mountainside, where from a hundred chasms and ravines, the torrents come roaring down the glens, streaking their slopes with threads of silver."

The Cuillin of Skye

Except for the ascent of Blaven and Sgurr nan Gillean in 1857, and that of Sgurr na Stri in 1859, I can find no record of any climbing in the Cuillin between Forbes's second ascent of Sgurr nan Gillean in 1845 and Nicolson's ascent in 1865. Almost certainly there were ascents during that twenty-year period, if not by tourists, then by shepherds or foresters, though Nicolson says that Skye then saw few strangers, except yachtsmen, bagmen and a stray geologist.

Nicolson's first ascent was in June 1865, when he was guided by the gamekeeper at Sligachan, son of Duncan MacIntyre with whom Professor Forbes had climbed. How could that man have guided him had he not been shown the route by his father? Possibly the tourist route up Sgurr nan Gillean was then well known to other natives of Skye. Naturally it was by that route Nicolson made the ascent. Let us be with him on the summit of Sgurr nan Gillean:

"It is undoubtedly a very solemn place to be in, and the slight suggestion of danger gives it an awful charm. In such places there is no poet whom I prefer to King David, who, among his other fine qualities, must certainly have been an accomplished mountaineer. If he had not been accustomed to go up and down rocky hills he would not have sung that glorious song:

> *I to the hills will lift mine eyes,*
> *From whence doth come mine aid.*
> *My safety cometh from the Lord,*
> *Who heaven and earth hath made;*
> *Thy foot he'll not let slide. . . .*

"In these days of Protoplasm and enlarged views it may seem childish to quote David as anything of an authority. But I am not ashamed to confess that in such a place as Sgurr nan Gillean, I actually derive some strength and comfort from that old-fashioned sentiment 'Thy foot he'll not let slide'. It's all very well to know that the gabbro on which you plant your foot is of such a chemical structure, and affords the most splendid footing, I know it and rejoice in the fact. But I also know, or at least believe, that it was not a blind and fatal force, but an intelligent person, that did in the beginning create the heavens and the earth that

26

did in due time order the upheaval of Sgurr nan Gillean, and that does at this hour watch over every creature of His that goes up and down its craggy sides. I have no notion that Providence will preserve me from death if I neglect the plain dictates of common sense and the inflexible laws of nature. But I have enough of the old unscientific belief to feel, on going up and down Sgurr nan Gillean, or any similar place, that the only power to keep my foot from sliding originates, not in a soulless force, but in a Paternal Mind. If Professors Tyndall and Huxley should consider me an ass for this, I don't care. I back David against them with great equanimity."

Not for Nicolson the tame descent of Sgurr nan Gillean by the way he had come. Always the explorer, he wanted something different, so proposed they should try the north-west ridge and go down Coir' a' Bhasteir. MacIntyre knew nothing of the route, but agreed. Nicolson took the lead, continued along the ridge, then made a "vermicular descent" by a chimney to the depths of the corrie, rounded the rocks and climbed to the summit of Bruach na Frithe. This clearly showed Nicolson's ability as a route-finder. At the very first go he had found the easiest way off this formidable ridge. Like a true mountaineer he was not content till he had also made the ascent by this new route, and this he did on his next visit to the island. There are now many and varied routes to the summit of Sgurr nan Gillean, and "Nicolson's Chimney" receives scant attention from modern cragsmen, yet that first traverse of his over unknown ground is of historic interest and there can be no doubt that his success encouraged him to explore the Cuillin far and wide.

In the years that followed he wandered among them, sometimes with a shepherd, sometimes with a like-minded companion, but often alone, and dismissed the opinion that "the best mountain views are got from below" as "a safe and easy doctrine".

A night out he does not mind, for has he not just seen

"Golden islets floating on the golden sky, their edges burning as the sun moved down, while up to the Zenith, the amber expanse is flecked with innumerable violet clouds. As the sun descends the gold becomes pink and then purple and the floating islets stretch in slender bars to the north. When the sun disappears the sky changes from flame to straw

27

colour and then to a delicate green, out of which presently shines the first twinkle of a star. The shadow of the great hills falls solemnly on the glassy sea."

It was after a night like that he writes:

> *The soft dewy steps of the gloaming*
> *Are climbing the sides of the Ben*
> *The last flush of light crowns with glory*
> *The Herdsman that watches the glen.*
> *Here wrapped in my plaid in the heather,*
> *I envy no monarch his bed:*
> *Come, dream of the hills and the Highlands*
> *And visit in slumber my head.*

He saw through a storm at Coruisk:

"What a sight was that seething cauldron and its black environment with the mists rolling down and flying up and winding about and struggling like persecuted ghosts . . . there leaped out of the grey turmoil the black head of some formidable peak, wildly defiant, and in a moment again it was hidden by the driving mist."

It was fitting that such a man should be the first to gain the highest point of the Cuillin in 1873. From Glen Brittle on a very stormy day he found his way to the lochan at the head of Coire Lagan and obtained out of the midst of driving mist a single glimpse of a great peak, one of the wildest objects he had ever seen.

The next day being fine, he decided to climb it, going first to Sgurr na Banachdich, which he had previously visited, then along the ridge to Sgurr Dearg. He passed by the Inaccessible Pinnacle and said "it might be possible with ropes and grappling irons to overcome it, but the achievement seems hardly worth the trouble". In the light of his magnificent ascent of Sgurr Dubh the following year, he might well have gained the summit of the Inaccessible had he tried it seriously, and so forestalled the Pilkington brothers.

On this occasion his mission was the great peak he had seen the previous day, and which now stood out sharp and clear across the corrie. With that perfect judgment he had shown elsewhere he hit off the route at once, descended into upper Coire Lagan and climbed up by what we now know as the Great Stone Shoot:

> "The climb up the other side of the corrie was stiff and warm and some judgment required to find a way and still more when it came to circumventing the peak. We did it however without much difficulty, one or two places were somewhat trying, requiring a good grip of hands and feet, but on the whole I have seen worse places."

There are really three peaks on the ridge which borders Coire Lagan to the south and at that time they were lumped together under the name Sgurr Sgumain. Now, most happily, that name is applied to the western and lesser peak, the central and highest point being called Sgurr Alasdair after him who first ascended it. (No. 10.)

Next year took place Nicolson's greatest effort—the first ascent of Sgurr Dubh. It was September. Nicolson and a friend had been visiting an artist at Loch Coruisk. Was it rashness to try a formidable peak at four in the afternoon when sunset was at seven? For others perhaps, not for Nicolson, who was by now a very experienced hillman; from a reading of his pocket barometer he judged that the weather would remain fair, and a full moon would give aid to him on his descent. (No. 13.)

They set off up the corrie between Sgurr Dubh and Gars-bheinn. Filled with a mass of enormous boulders it is one of the roughest corries in Skye. Halfway up they had to seek shelter when rain came on and mist hid the ridge above. Nicolson trusted the barometer and believed that the mist would have cleared away before they reached the top as, in fact, it did. They had difficult climbing towards the summit, which they reached at seven o'clock at night. The sun was now sinking, so they had to commence the descent at once, hoping twilight would last to the bottom of the corrie on the other side. About halfway down they got to a steep wall, where Nicolson brought into use his substitute for the modern climber's rope—a plaid rug which he always carried with him and of which he wrote:

> "With the help of a belt it can be made into a full-dress for a man, it is the best and lightest of wraps by day and serves for bed clothes at night; it can be used as a bag; it will serve as a sail for a boat; it is valuable as a rope for rock climbing; it can be turned into a curtain, an awning, a carpet, a cushion, a hammock. Its uses are, in fact, endless

29

and as a garment it has this superiority over every other, that 'there's room in it for twa'."

This is how he used it when descending Sgurr Dubh:

"My companion, being the lighter man, stood above, with his heels well set in the rock, holding the plaid by which I let myself down the chasm. Having got footing I rested my back against the rock down which my lighter friend let himself slide till he rested on my shoulder. This little piece of gymnastics we had to practise several times before we got to the bottom of the glen above Coruisk. From eight till half past ten we descended in almost total darkness, for, though the moon rose about nine and we could see her mild glory in the depths below, we were all the way down in the deep shadow of the peak behind us. Most of the way was among shelving ledges of rock, and at one place it seemed there was no going further for there was no apparent outlet except down a dark gully over which a stream descended in a small cascade."

They managed to wriggle down the wet rock and finally reached easier ground. Both admitted that they had never in the same space of time gone through so much severe bodily exercise and both had their finger-tips skinned from contact with the rough-grained rock. It was with thankful hearts that they got into the full flood of moonlight in the valley above Coruisk.

Even after that Nicolson tried a short cut over Druim nam Ramh to Harta Corrie. Some way up difficulties became too severe to face in the dark, so he retreated right down to Coruisk, found the usual route over Drum Hain and thence to Sligachan, which the two heroes reached at 3 a.m.

Few climbers of today would venture the descent from Sgurr Dubh to Coir' an Lochain in darkness and without a rope. For Nicolson it was absolutely unknown ground; to find a way down safely set the seal to his fame as a mountaineer.

When Nicolson first knew Skye tourists were few and far between, but by 1870 the island had become known, while ten years later it had become fashionable and the available accommodation not nearly enough for its visitors. The influx of tourists was due partly to the opening of the railway to Strome in 1870, which made for much easier access, and partly to the series of articles on Skye which Nicolson contributed to *Good Words* in 1875. For

The Past

Good Words was a national magazine, edited by Dr Norman MacLeod, Queen Victoria's chaplain, and had a very influential circulation.

It is indeed a pity Nicolson never attempted a book on Skye, for his articles read well today, and he was certainly a much better writer than he was given credit for in his lifetime. He foresaw Skye as a supreme attraction for tourists, and as long ago as 1872 was suggesting that a bridge might easily be built across the narrow stretch of water between Kyle of Lochalsh and Kyleakin. The subject is still appropriate though the ferry is now much more efficient than formerly. He was greatly attracted by the unrivalled position of Camasunary, as thousands have been since that time, and thought of Skye as the Oberland of Scotland with, at Camasunary, the

> Grand Hôtel de Blaveinn
> Grand Hôtel des Cuchullins
> Grand Hôtel et Pension de Camasunary

Camasunary is still the same as in Nicolson's time. There is still no accommodation for tourists.

Again and again Nicolson told us that Skye weather was always at its best during the months of May and June, and pointed out that a day in June is equal to a day and a half in August or September, darkness being limited to an hour between midnight and 1 a.m.—"the rich gloaming still lingers tenderly in the north-west till bars of yellow light are seen in the east heralding the dawn".

Unfortunately his advice could not overcome conservatism of holiday habits and for many, many years after his time the autumn was considered the season for Skye, with the result that the island got quite an undeserved reputation for rain, but Nicolson stoutly claims "in a competitive examination for rain I would back Greenock or Fort William against Skye any day".

Nicolson, too, was the first to prove that it was a mistake to suppose that the beauties of the Highlands were not appreciated by the natives, and that the taste for scenery is an affair of cultivation. The proof? The finest poems of Duncan Ban MacIntyre are descriptive. He painted every feature of the mountains with the hands of a master—"for him the love of nature and scenery was as little the product of fashion and teaching as was his delight in the warbling of the birds and the belling of the red deer".

Nicolson, like Collie who was to follow him, had no patience with those who kept meticulous records of their times up and down mountains and gave them

31

a right good telling off with his entry in the Sligachan Visitors' Book in 1872.

[Handwritten entry in Sligachan Visitors' Book]

NICOLSON'S ENTRY IN SLIGACHAN VISITORS' BOOK *

Every other year he returned to Skye and when he gave up climbing he was still supremely happy at Sligachan. In 1885 he writes:

"After an unwilling absence of three years, I have come back to this, my favourite haunt in the island I love best, and leave it, as usual with reluctance. I have praised this house often, recommended it to everyone requiring advice as the best hotel nor only in Skye, but in the Western Isles. Here, as before, I feel really at home; here a day is worth two in most places."

He praises everything, even the rain, then adds a note deploring the "unspeakable track" through Glen Sligachan and suggesting it could be easily improved by removing the stones which obstruct it and making the bogs more passable.

* The following is a translation of the Gaelic verse:

House, man and wife better than I've found here
I know not throughout the Isle of mist;
My blessings on them! As long as they live here
The Clan MacDonald will never lose renown.

32

This entry led to amusing backchat. A critic added: "Mr Nicolson is evidently getting old and *garulous*"—to which Nicolson retorted, pleading guilty to the former but not to the latter even if his critic could spell!

Often Nicolson added verses in his mother tongue:

> *Mo bheannochd air an tigh so,*
> *'S na bheil ann,*
> *Fear 'us bean an tighe*
> *'Us a chlann.*

> *(My blessing on this house*
> *And those who are therein,*
> *The guidman and his wife*
> *And their children).*

While his last entry shortly before his death consisted of the lines now so often quoted:

> *Jerusalem, Athens and Rome,*
> *I would see them before I die:*
> *But I'd rather not see any one of these three*
> *Than be exiled for ever from Skye.*

It is as a mountaineer we honour him here. Science came first with Forbes and guides went with him. Nicolson opened the door wide; he was the first real mountaineer and explorer among the Cuillin. His descent of the Coruisk face of Sgurr Dubh in darkness was the finest thing done in climbing in Britain up till that time, and might well be reckoned as notable as Whymper's first ascent of the Matterhorn.

He brought a new conception to the climbing game, and to his critics roundly declared: "The loss of life is a small thing compared with the full and free exercise of our powers and the cultivation of a bold adventurous spirit; and any nation which has ceased to think so is on the fair road to decay and degradation."

The Climbers Arrive

PEDESTRIAN CLIMBERS

BEFORE the time of a building at Sligachan, there was an inn at Sconser near the site of the present Sconser Lodge. This inn had its place in history. Here it was that the young Clanranald met The MacLeod and Sir Alexander MacDonald in 1745 and tried to persuade them to join Prince Charlie's cause. Both stayed "out" and the rising was more or less doomed from the beginning. This inn still functioned till the middle of the nineteenth century.

Before the bridge was built across the river the original inn at Sligachan was near a ford about half a mile south of the present site. Road-making in Skye was first carried out between 1811 and 1817 and the first inn by the bridge is subsequent to this, probably about 1830.

Lesingham Smith was made comfortable there, and the reputation for comfort and hospitality has endured through all the years and all the alterations since then. To begin with it had comparatively few visitors and almost all sailed from Oban to Portree. As recently as 1862 we find a tourist taking a horse with him to Skye and meeting a landlord at Sligachan who had the utmost contempt for the weather-glass: "Deed, sir, I never seen the glass hae muckle effec' on the weather in these parts."

The influx of visitors started after that. By 1875 the demand for accommodation was such that a corrugated iron building of seven bedrooms and a smoking-room was added. In this smoking-room all the climbers of the classic period foregathered; indeed it lasted till 1934. There were further additions in 1905 and 1927, till finally in 1934 the old smoking-room was pulled down and replaced by a new wing with the palatial lounge we know today.

34

The first Visitor's Book available is from 1869 and almost four hundred names appear in that season, many of them in perfect copper-plate writing such as we seldom see nowadays, and the majority from furth of Scotland. There are a great many references as to the comfort of the hotel and the kindliness of Mr and Mrs MacDonald who were then the proprietors. A stimulus was given by a visit from Royalty, the name "Arthur" (Duke of Connaught) appearing in June 10th of that year.

The comments on the weather are various and J. M. Forrester of Glasgow breaks into verse:

Fair weather without, good fare within,
I'll ne'er forget Glen Sligachan Inn,

which a later visitor alters to read:

Foul weather without, guid whusky within,
I'll aye remember Sligachan Inn.

The first entry relating to the mountains is by R. Abbay of Wadham on August 27th: "Climbed Sgurr nan Gillean alone in a little less than three hours and found no part dangerous even when mist came on. The upper two thirds is over large blocks of stone, the view on all sides is grand and certainly ought to be seen by every pedestrian."

The only others who accepted the invitation that year were William and Peter Denny, the shipbuilders from Dumbarton, who record on September 1st: "Climbed Sgurr nan Gillean in five minutes less than two hours from leaving Sligachan Inn. The ascent is rough but not difficult."

Even in 1870 it was a case of returning "again yet and again", for a tourist boasts of the third visit within five years, while another hankers for the delights of civilisation by bemoaning the lack of a daily paper.

In July and August of that year, three parties made ascents of Sgurr nan Gillean without guides, these being H. and J. McDougall of Dublin, George Grieve of Burntisland, and W. H. Kidston and G. B. and J. C. MacLure of Glasgow.

That the mountain was not without danger was proved in September 1870, when a young man from Liverpool lost his life. Two had set off for the summit, one returned, and the other went on alone. He gained the peak, left his name in a bottle by the cairn, fell and was killed while descending. The book records it:

The Cuillin of Skye

Don't tempt the grim old hills without a guide:
John Thom did this: the same day he died.
The hills have secrets that no tourist knows:
He risks his life who solitary goes.

There was no further climbing that year. Maybe that example led to increasing care, and it is good to know that among the Cuillin, the most difficult mountains in Britain, there was not another fatality for fifty years.

In 1871 the record-breakers were at it again. J. J. Owen, J. Baumann, J. P. Cundill and J. R. Hall, all army officers, note: "Got to summit of Sgurr nan Gillean in 1 hour 50 minutes from hotel (no guide). Had to walk hard to do it in this time"; while, in a pencilled comment below: "the captain's watch must have stopped on the way". This party also claimed "the ascent of the sharp peak opposite Sgurr na Stri. Rather difficult in places and no traces of previous ascent, built a cairn on top." This may have been a first ascent of Sgurr Dubh Beag. Few, however, were so adventurous, the following entry being more typical of the tourist's mood:

"Started at 8.10 a.m. this morning for the top of Sgurr nan Gillean and not without considerable effort reached there at 10.50 a.m. Put name in bottle and made tracks down with a thankful heart, having, however, lost our way coming off the most difficult peak on the top, had some uneasiness before finding it. Not advisable to go unless strong and sure footed, in nothing but good weather and with a guide who thoroughly knows the way. Ye who would behold the terrible works of the Creator— go and see these awful rocks—it will fill your heart with fear and may make you a better man than John Dunbar."

By 1872 the accident had been forgotten and there where no less than ten ascents with and without guides. Not one of the parties thought of trying any of the other peaks, though some of them ventured further by descending to Harta Corrie and including Loch Coruisk in the same excursion.

A minor problem often gave worry:

Did ae body ken
Sic an awfu glen
Wi' its mosses and mires and ridges?
But ainst within
The Sligachan Inn
We forgive them a' but the MIDGES!

36

In 1873 a bolder spirit arrived. Professor Knight reached Skye after several seasons of Alpine climbing, including the Matterhorn and other famous mountains. He had been told of unclimbed peaks in Skye, and had set his heart on a first ascent. Like most other tourists his first effort was Sgurr nan Gillean by the tourist route, and his guide, one by name Macpherson, was horrified when the Professor suggested climbing the peak immediately to the north of the summit which we know as Knight's Peak, or the fourth pinnacle of Sgurr nan Gillean. Persuasion of the pocket had to be used before Macpherson would agree and even then he proved to be more a hindrance than a help. On the way up Knight had sometimes to pull the guide up after him, and on the way down give him a shoulder on which to rest his feet. It was enough for Macpherson: he declared with a sigh that he "would never go up that mountain never no more".

The little climb had merely whetted Knight's appetite and he tried to persuade the guide to accompany him on a longer expedition. This was to be in Alpine style, with two porters in addition to Macpherson, and they would be away for three days, sleep out among the mountains, and climb a new peak each day. Macpherson was interested till the Professor mentioned that the party would be roped together to enable them to go up and down steep places. Up till then a rope had never been used in rock climbing in Skye, and the idea of being tied on to one scared Macpherson altogether. He, like certain early guides in the Alps, knew one route up one peak. That was enough; he had no desire to venture in the unknown.

Nowadays Knight's ascent and descent of the fourth pinnacle from the gap between it and Sgurr nan Gillean is but a small part of the classic Pinnacle Ridge climb and the first part of it to be climbed. The thousands who follow the trail of hobnails over the four pinnacles think little of it. But they are secure in the knowledge that generations of climbers have been over that particular route, and that it is quite straightforward. Knight had no such knowledge; the unknown, the uncertainty, the possibility of loose rock must always add many degrees of difficulty even without the problem of an unreliable companion. So that Professor Knight, though his contribution is slight, is entitled to a worthy place in the development of climbing among the Cuillin. (No. 22.)

One wishes Knight could have teamed up with Nicolson. What a pair they would have made! Had they done so and had sufficient time they might well have conquered most of the peaks then unclimbed.

There is another even more exciting "might-have-been". The Pilkington brothers were in Skye in 1872, when they spent their time fishing and did no climbing. Suppose they had been a year later and had fallen in with Nicolson and Knight. The possibilities of such a quartette were almost unlimited. The Pilkingtons came and departed, giving little thought to the Cuillin, and the chance was lost.

The tourists, artists and geologists were more numerous than the climbers. Almost every artist of note had to paint Coruisk, while amateur efforts were legion. After Turner came Horatio MacCulloch, who painted the Cuillin and Coruisk on four visits spaced over twenty years, and MacWhirter, Alfred Williams and many others of lesser name. There seems to have been an endless sale for "Coruisks". In 1879 two Scottish artists, Murray and MacDonald, stayed for two months at Coruisk in what was little more than a tin box, painted industriously, exhibiting and selling the results in Edinburgh the following winter.

Coruisk was still the lion; many the comments on the dourness of the Skye ponies which took cavalcades of tourists through Glen Sligachan. An American visitor embraces everything: "Liked the hotel, the proprietor, the guide, Angus Macpherson, the ducks, grouse and deer that he showed me; also the lochs, the moors and the crags"; while a German gives only the criticism, complaining bitterly of the boatman's charge of eight shillings to row him from Camasunary to Loch Scavaig.

Robert Buchanan, the poet, puts it poetically: "The Cuillin Hills are the Temple of Ossian and the Temple has two portals, Sligachan and Scavaig." To him Sligachan Inn was the cleanest, snuggest, cheapest little place of the sort in all the Highlands of Scotland. Buchanan's "Coruskin Lyrics" convey something of the spirit of the place, but his prose description is an echo of MacCulloch: " . . . Surrounded on every side by rocks and precipices, totally without vegetation and towering one sheer plane of livid rock. The brooding desolation is there for ever . . . perpetual twilight . . . unbroken darkness . . . melancholy marked it for its own . . . the walls of livid rock remain casting perpetual darkness downwards." No thought had he of penetrating that "awful place", where now almost every surrounding crag bears the traces of hobnailed boots.

All the visitors of the nineteenth century were impressed by Coruisk and its majestic surroundings. All but one—Malcolm Ferguson—who thought that, had it not been publicised by Sir Walter Scott it would have remained unnoticed, and to whom the little Loch na Creitheach under the shadow of

Blaven was infinitely more picturesque. Up till today no other traveller or climber has agreed with Ferguson.

THE ALPINE CLUB

Charles Pilkington was twenty-two when he made his first visit to Skye with his elder brother, Alfred, in 1872, though Charles had already climbed the Pillar Rock in Lakeland, quite a feat in those days. They spent all their time fishing and made no ascents.

For the next few years Charles, with his younger brother, Lawrence, visited Switzerland regularly and by 1877 were able to dispense with guides. Theirs was the first party deliberately to plan guideless tours in the Alps and carry them through successfully, the greatest of these being the ascent of the Meije in 1879. When they returned to Skye in 1880 they were among the foremost mountaineers of their time. Even so, it was not the Cuillin which brought them to Skye. Shooting and fishing were still their objectives. The grouse they sought were not in evidence, the rivers were too low and the trout would not rise.

Something had to be done. They tried a frontal attack on Sgurr nan Gillean, and "were deflated and felt rather small" when it defeated them. This defeat on homeland hills after their great efforts in the Alps made them change their opinion and they showed a much greater respect for the Cuillin thereafter. They retrieved themselves the following day when they gained the summit of Sgurr nan Gillean by the west ridge. To show their mettle they had to climb something which had never been climbed before, so it is not surprising they were attracted to the Inaccessible Pinnacle, that weird obelisk which juts up from the ridge near the summit of Sgurr Dearg. The approach was made from Coruisk via Bealach Coire na Banachdich. Nowadays the ascent of the Inaccessible by the east ridge is comparatively simple, though one is always conscious of the great exposure. For the pioneers it was vastly different. Loose rock abounded, and all this had to be prised out and hurled down to gain safe holding. The Pilkingtons described it as one of the noisiest climbs they had ever made. "The very pinnacle seemed to vibrate with indignation." The brothers also climbed Blaven during this visit, but details are lacking. Charles Pilkington was one of the luckiest of mortals. In three visits of ten days' duration his party experienced wonderful sunny weather each time. (No. 17.)

Certain records tell of an unnamed shepherd who made a solo ascent of the

Inaccessible in 1881, while others state that no native of Skye other than John Mackenzie had made the ascent prior to 1886. It may possibly have been John who was the unnamed one.

After 1881 it remained unclimbed for two years, till Horace Walker, Eustace Hulton and Lawrence Pilkington visited Skye in 1883. This time, not having the lucky Charles with them, they learned the vagaries of Skye weather. It rained almost every day for three weeks. Even on the moors there were difficulties. On one occasion they stepped lightly over a burn in the morning, to discover a raging torrent when they returned in the evening, so that they had to climb high up the corrie and struggle across shoulder to shoulder to prevent themselves being swept away by the force of the water. Many expeditions had to be cancelled; even so they managed to make the first ascent of the highest of four tops of Bidein Druim nan Ramh and the third ascent of the Inaccessible.

For Lawrence, alas, it was almost the last of his climbing days. An accident the following year made further climbing impossible, though he loved and frequented the mountains till the end. A poet, whose slim volumes deserve wider knowledge, his verses on the Cuillin, sharp and clear, seem to typify the jagged pinnacles:

> *Oh for the hills of Skye,*
> *With storm-wracked cliffs on high:*
> *Where sunset's streaming fire*
> *Drapes Sgurr nan Gillean's spire:*
> *Where climbers gladly greet*
> *Rock safe for hand and feet,*
> *On which dear life to trust*
> *However fierce the gust,*
> *Oh for the hills of Skye,*
> *Dark Coolin hills of Skye.*

Such doings were bound to attract W. P. Haskett Smith, that great pioneer of Lakeland climbing. He did not think much of the Inaccessible, ascending in four minutes, spending two minutes on the top and descending in six minutes! His ascent and descent were by the long easy route, and he considered it called for care rather than for skill. In the same year (1886) A. H. Stocker and A. G. Parker went one better by ascending the Inaccessible by the short and steep western side. This is quite a different proposition from the east ridge, and, as will be seen in the photographs (No. 15), is almost vertical. The holds, however, are good, the only real difficulty being the problem of getting from a narrow ledge on to a sloping platform about five feet higher, which is apt to be slippery when wet, as the Pinnacle is of basalt and not of rough gabbro. Most folk find it easier to ascend than to descend by this side, and for descent a doubled rope is often used (Nos. 67, 68). This party made the first traverse of the Pinnacle from west to east.

Charles Pilkington came to Skye again in May 1887, together with Horace Walker and James Heelis, and had perfect weather throughout. How modern climbers must envy them! Almost every day they trod where never foot had trod before.

Sgurr nan Gillean, as usual, started off the programme; then they climbed Bidein Druim nan Ramh by much the same route as the 1883 party. With John Mackenzie as their "handyman" they moved over to Glen Brittle, "A Riffel for our Zermatt", where they camped in the unfurnished drawing-room of the house, Glen Brittle then being a sheep farm and unlet.

Next day they made for Coire Lagan to examine Sgurr Alasdair, whose northern top was then unclimbed and unnamed. They scaled it by the precipitous and difficult face at the head of the corrie. Charles was the leader and it was very fitting that the peak should be named Sgurr Thearlaich in his honour. From it they descended to the top of the great Stone Shoot, traversed over Sgurr Alasdair and Sgurr Sgumain and down the ridge to the glen.

During that excursion they noticed with interest a graceful and nameless peak at the head of the corrie and between Sgurr Thearlaich and Sgurr Dearg. The possibility of another first ascent brought them back to Coire Lagan the very next day. First they made for Sgurr Dearg and traversed the Inaccessible from west to east in the footsteps of Stocker and Parker, then climbed the nameless peak from the col between it and Sgurr Dearg—"a fine easy climb with precipitous rocks on either side of the ridge". Of course John Mackenzie was with them and they laughingly suggested the peak should be named Pic Mackenzie. Fortunately, and very justly, the name survives as Sgurr Mhic Coinnich, ever to remind us of that great guide. (No. 20.)

Charles remarked what a grand climb it would be to continue from Sgurr Mhic Coinnich over Sgurr Thearlaich, Sgurr Alasdair and Sgurr Sgumain. This ridge walk from Sgurr Dearg to Sgurr Sgumain, now called the round of Coire Lagan, is undoubtedly one of the finest day's outings in Skye.

The same party also made a first ascent of the west face of Sgurr a' Ghreadaidh and of Clach Glas and Sgurr na h-Uamha. All three were entranced

41

with the magnificence of the climbing and agreed that "we may have seen grander forms in the Alps, and as beautiful colouring in Italy and we may have seen views of equal loveliness, but we know of none to beat it for beauty of colour combined with grandeur and variety of form".

The Pilkington party was a very careful one, and roped up for all the climbs, so that Charles was considerably pained when he found that someone had added, to his careful account in the Sligachan Visitors' Book:—"Ropes all the time!" and himself added: "This remark is heartless and need not have been added by Mr H. C. Hart."

The rollicking Mr Hart from Dublin never bothered to use a rope among the Cuillin. Later in 1887 he put in some very long days with John Mackenzie. One was from Sgurr nan Gillean by way of Am Basteir, Bruach na Frithe, Bidein Druim nan Ramh and Sgurr a' Mhadaidh to Sgurr a' Ghreadaidh. His best effort was from Sgurr na Banachdich, over Sgurr Dearg, to traverse the Inaccessible from west to east, thence over Sgurr Mhic Coinnich, Sgurr Thearlaich and Sgurr Alasdair. He was able to keep to the crest of the ridge, except for the descent from Sgurr Mhic Coinnich to the col beyond. Hence he made the first round of Coire Lagan as suggested by Pilkington and also the first unroped traverse of the Inaccessible. On this Pinnacle Hart gave John a leg-up, John wearing ordinary shepherd's boots with smooth iron toe-plates and heel-plates. When Hart stated in the Visitors' Book that he used no ropes at any time, a later climber added: "A rope with a noose at the end and a long drop would have suited this idiot."

Hart has another claim to fame in that he it was who first found *Arabis Alpina* in Coire na Creiche. This rare plant does not occur anywhere else in Britain. It is still very much of a find for the botanist and about five locations have been noted in the Cuillin.

In February 1888 the *Alpine Journal* published its first article about the Cuillin of Skye from the pen of Charles Pilkington and brought the peaks very vividly to the notice of climbers in the south. In 1890 we find him organising a large party—all members of the Alpine Club. This consisted of Clinton Dent, Herman Wooley, Geoffrey Hastings, Horace Walker and W. C. Slingsby—all of them names known and honoured in the history of world mountaineering. Dent, Walker, Pilkington and Slingsby each, in turn, became President of the Alpine Club. Slingsby was the father of Norwegian mountaineering, while Wooley climbed in the Caucasus and Hastings in the Himalaya.

Charles led them up the Pinnacle Ridge of Sgurr nan Gillean to start off with. Next day a party went off to Clach Glas and Blaven, Slingsby and Hastings making a new route up the latter, while Charles took his wife up the Inaccessible Pinnacle, she being the first woman to reach its summit. Determined to show the others every variety of Skye climbing, he then introduced them to ridge walking, making first for Sgurr a' Mhadaidh and then continuing along the ridge over Sgurr a' Ghreadaidh and Sgurr na Banachdich with the Inaccessible as their goal. The Pinnacle they traversed from west to east before descending to Glen Brittle—a perfect route for an introduction to ridge walking in Skye.

Another great day was when they traversed over Sgurr Sgumain, Sgurr Alasdair and Sgurr Thearlaich in the hope of following the ridge to Sgurr Dubh, only to find the route "impracticable". They do not mention the cause, but it was the now famous Thearlaich-Dubh gap. They returned to the col between Sgurr Alasdair and Sgurr Sgumain, from which they traversed to Coir' a' Ghrunnda and reached the ridge again at Bealach Coir' an Lochain. Two of the party then climbed Sgurr Dubh, while the other two toiled through the boulder field which leads down to Coruisk. But that is one of the roughest corries in Skye and they were no quicker than the climbers who joined them near the loch.

Why make for Coruisk when Sligachan was their base? There was a very special attraction for weary climbers at Coruisk at that time and for years thereafter. Mr Alfred Williams, the painter, had a rude shelter between Loch Coruisk and Loch Scavaig and always gave a princely welcome, providing from out of a hole, bottles of beer, cold beef and other luxuries. Long hot days in the Cuillin produce a terrific thirst; no wonder that climbers so often put Coruisk on their round.

On this occasion Williams was absent and the party, knowing the secret cache, refreshed themselves. At Sligachan in the evening they met the artist, and the President said: "Ah, Williams, you are a man to be envied! You're the richer by the heartfelt thanks of four weary, thirsty climbers, but (*sotto voce*) the poorer by six bottles of beer." One of the climbers also claimed Williams as a better man than Moses, for whereas Moses had but produced water from the rock, Williams could produce beer.

Williams made a great many visits to Skye, was ever helpful to and naturally very popular among climbers. He was a great lover of mountain scenery and had also painted among the Himalaya and the Alps. He did a great many paintings of the Cuillin and also made the first really accurate drawing of the

43

Cuillin from end to end. A lithograph from this was used to illustrate the article in the *Alpine Journal* by Charles Pilkington already mentioned.

Perhaps the brightest exploit of this party was the ascent of the Basteir Gorge by Hastings, Slingsby and Hopkinson. This is a great chasm which separates Sgurr nan Gillean from Sgurr a' Bhasteir. Others had already tried and failed and the party was not quite certain as to the cause of the failure. Afterwards, from notes supplied by Slingsby, Clinton Dent wrote an account of the climb, which is here given in full, as it is so vastly different from the manner in which climbs are described in club journals today:

"The actual obstruction was a matter of uncertainty. Very soon, however, when the party were well in the gorge the nature of the difficulty was disclosed and turned out to be a pool of water some thirty to forty feet in length and twelve feet in width, averaging probably about ten feet in depth. A tarn of this nature forms a very pretty feature in a mountain picture but a somewhat unexpected obstacle to the mountaineer; howbeit as the party seem to have been going a sort of steeplechase a water jump was not much out of place. It is deeply regretted that the ubiquitous photographer was not present on the occasion. My information is limited really to the notes supplied and I can but give the bare facts of the climb; a photographer might have been able to record some of the bare facts much more graphically. On each side of the little tarn the rocks were perpendicular, a term that in mountaineering literature signifies anything from difficult to impossible; at any rate they were sheer enough to be pronounced impracticable. At the head of the pool a little waterfall some twenty feet high completed the picture. A huge rock which at some time or another had fallen from the side of the mountain had become wedged in the steep bed of the little stream and other loose stones were piled on the top of it. The big boulder projected about ten feet over the pool. It was necessary, therefore, in the first place, to get to the head of the pool, and in the second to turn the boulder. A bold attempt by Hastings to find a way by a little ledge, while still observing the ordinary mountaineering proprieties in the matter of costume, proved fruitless. After some ingenious climbing he was pounded and it seemed possible for a minute or two, to the great delectation of his companions that, in the words of the Portuguese dialogue book, "he could not nor to go further neither to put back". The alternative route back lay through the pool and those who were in a

23. Looking across to Sgurr Dearg from the top of the Great Stone Shoot of Sgurr Alasdair.
The nearer pinnacle is An Stac, while the farther one, the Inaccessible Pinnacle is
clearly shown as over-topping the summit ridge of Sgurr Dearg, Bealach Coire Lagan
is on the ridge at the extreme right

1   2   3   4   5   6   7   8   9   10   11   12   13   14 15 16 1

24. The main ridge of the Cuillin from Clach Glas

1. Ridge to Gars bheinn	2. Sgurr a' Choire Bhig
3. Sgurr nan Eag	4. Sgurr Dubh Mor
5. Sgurr Alasdair	6. Sgurr Mhic Coinnich
7. Sgurr Dearg	8. Sgurr na Banachdich
9. Sgurr Thormaid	10. Sgurr a' Ghreadaidh
11. Sgurr a' Mhadaidh	12. Bidein Druim nan Ramh
13. An Caisteal with Sgurr na h-Uamha just below it	
14. Bruach na Frithe	15. Sgurr a' Fhionn Choire
16. Am Basteir and Tooth	17. Sgurr nan Gillean

Lochan Athain is in the foreground and the track from Sligachan to Camasunary is on the near side of it. The long ridge (Druim nan Ramh) running south from Bidein is well seen and Loch Coruisk lies between it and the main ridge position of safety watched with interest to see which way might be selected. By means of some ingenious movements described by the spectators rather contemptuously as a wriggle he succeeded in rejoining his companions without taking an involuntary bath. Meanwhile the others had adopted a costume more suitable for the emergency and stood like yellow primroses on the brim. Then the leader plunged boldly in and swam to the head of the pool. So far the route was simple enough but a more painful exercise consisted in climbing the rock to the top of the waterfall. The performance is described as having been more instructive from an anatomical point of view than graceful. The rope was now thrown up and Slingsby and Hopkinson as true gymnasts followed. Even now the difficulties were not at an end for, a few feet further up, another tarn was found which, however, it was possible to ford though the party was waist deep in the water. From the upper pool to the end of the gorge the obstacles were less and the party soon emerged into the very head of Coir' a' Bhasteir. It is difficult in these days to discover any novelty and unwise to claim originality in anything whatever but I can recall no other recorded occasion on which any party ascended a mountain by water— since the days of Noah."

This account puzzled many folk, for it gives the impression that they completed their climb in a state of nature. Sunbathing among the Cuillin is one matter; climbing totally unclad is entirely another, and anyone who knows the rough texture of the gabbro and the airiness of the ridges will shudder at the very thought. Slingsby later explained how Hastings plunged in, swam across the pool and climbed the waterfall on to the overhanging rock. The others jammed all clothes into a rucksack and tried to throw a rope to the shivering Hastings. After many unsuccessful attempts they at last managed to do so. The rucksack was fastened on and hauled over. Slingsby and Hopkinson then swam over, climbed the waterfall and donned their clothes above.

Up till today there is no record of such an exploit being repeated. Nor is it likely, as Harold Raeburn showed that the ascent could be made avoiding the waterfall pitch by climbing up the right wall.

Charles Pilkington complained of a "magnificent and complicated system of mistakes in the Ordnance Survey map unequalled in the British Isles", and himself did something to remedy that defect. A considerable artist, especially with water-colour, he also drew a map of the Cuillin, very much more detailed

45

and accurate than Forbes's eye sketch. This was reproduced and used by climbers for many years till it was superseded by the complete and accurate Ordnance Survey map.

Sixty years ago Clinton Dent gave his opinion of Skye climbing and it still holds true:

> "To every one of the peaks there are many lines of attack which seem promising, but which may lead the inexperienced climber into very formidable difficulties indeed. In any attempt to make a new route up a peak the utmost precaution should be taken with loose stones. As time goes on and the mountaineering in Skye becomes more popular the faces may be more swept and garnished and already a greater part of the range has been got in order. The weathering of the rocks is the chief cause of their extraordinary local variation as regards firmness. The rocks must nowhere be treated with contempt. Attempts to find new routes to ascend by untried buttresses and walls should be considered in detail as carefully as in the Alps and a rope should invariably be taken. Even a slight deviation from a recognised track may lead the climber to places where a slip might easily be fatal."

Nicolson opened the door to the Cuillin, the Pilkington party entered the Kingdom. Others were quick to follow. W. E. Corlett and E. Kidson were the most enterprising of the guideless parties and during the seasons 1889, 1890 and 1891 repeated most of the ascents of the A.C. group.

In 1889, also, Cameron Swan was one of the first to have experience of the Cuillin when snowbound. He found the ascent of Bruach na Frithe much easier because of the foothold given by soft snow and used a photographic tripod as an alpenstock.

However, the true pioneers of snow climbing were T. C. Porter and H. F. W. Tatham of Eton College. For five Easters from 1889 they were at Sligachan, being reinforced by Claude Benson during their last three visits. Altogether they made snow ascents of all the peaks bar Sgurr na h-Uamba, Sgurr Thearlaich, Sgurr Mhic Coinnich, Sgurr Dubh na Da Bheinn, Sgurr Dubh Mor and Clach Glas.

It is curious to note how much rock climbing was done in Skye before the great rock faces in Glencoe and on Ben Nevis were explored, though the latter two areas are much easier of access from the south. Even in Skye, with the exception of Nicolson and Knight and others who will be mentioned, Scottish climbers did not come into the game till after the formation of the Scottish Mountaineering Club. Before considering that phase we must take stock of two other great figures of the golden age whom many, with good reason, claim should share the premier position among climbers in the Cuillin for all time.

NORMAN AND JOHN

The early climbers, following Alpine practice, engaged a porter or guide and there were more available at Sligachan fifty years ago than at present. Shepherds knew the passes well and Nicolson tells of Angus MacRae of Glen Brittle who had a peculiar style of walk, a sort of amble, and "seemed to glide up the hillside like a cloud".

Professor Knight's experience with Angus Macpherson was not reassuring, but Angus, after accompanying Nicolson on several excursions did venture on other routes and latterly showed some boldness. In 1879 he led a party of three up the Basteir Corrie of Sgurr nan Gillean towards Nicolson's Chimney, which "gave rise to a long consultation". Angus had learned from Nicolson the technique of the plaid rug and carried a long one with him plus a strong staff six feet in length. With the aid of the staff the plaid was hitched over a spike of rock. By this means Angus drew himself up, prospected the route ahead and declared it would be possible to go on. He then planted himself firmly, let down the plaid and pulled up each of the three tourists in turn, whence they reached the summit without difficulty.

However, the first man who could properly be called a rock-climbing guide was John Mackenzie. He was born in 1856 in a croft at Sconser under the shadow of Glamaig and three miles from Sligachan. At the age of ten he climbed Sgurr nan Gillean, and when fourteen made the first ascent of Sgurr a' Ghreadaidh with Mr Tribe. With the increasing number of visitors to Sligachan John's fame soon became known, and he took many of them up Sgurr nan Gillean. He was with the Pilkingtons on that memorable day when they made the first ascent of the Inaccessible, but though they offered to take him up, he said he would wait till another day. John, you see, was still learning his trade and was content to watch the first experts with whom he had climbed. A year later he climbed it alone. In 1883 he was with Lawrence Pilkington's party when they made the third ascent of the Inaccessible. These three ascents were by the east ridge. John's first time up the west side was with R. C. Broomfield in 1886 after the effort by Stocker and Parker, and Charles Pilkington tells of the third ascent of this side in 1887 when they offered to take John up with them. "Oh, yes," was his ready reply. "Off went his boots and we tied him on to the rope. I believe his greatest anxiety for some time had been that we might send him round with the luggage to the other side and not give him the chance of a climb."

As has been noted, John led this steep side unroped with H. C. Hart later the same year, and he and several other climbers pointed out that John's boots were not suitable for rock climbing, which makes his efforts all the finer. Of course there were other guides, John's brother Murdo and, later, his nephews, Archie and Donald. All three were capable climbers but were content with ordinary routes; none of them achieved such a standard of climbing as John did and none of them took part in first ascents.

By 1889 Clinton Dent was writing that John

"may be without hesitation recommended most strongly as a guide. It is very easy to mistake the way in bad weather and his local knowledge is invaluable. In addition he is a capital climber, takes great interest in all modern refinements of new routes and variations, and is an excellent companion."

Such the opinion of the expert, while a beginner writes:

"This had been my first experience of climbing and I am much indebted to John Mackenzie for giving me such an enjoyable time and so much instruction. Both as guide and companion I can only re-echo all the good things that others have said of him—especially as to finding new virtues every day."

An incident of 1893 got wide publicity in the press. Mr Walter Greg left Sligachan for Camasunary, intending to go round the coast to Loch Scavaig, then return by Loch Coruisk and Glen Sligachan. He did not return that night; large search parties were out for two days before finding him. His route meant crossing the "Bad Step" near Loch Scavaig, which was described in the *Daily Telegraph* as

"a spot where the rocks fall so abruptly into the sea that you can only pass along a sharp and narrow ridge, where you must go sideways with the feet against the edge and the back against the cliffs. The sea foams and thunders sixty feet beneath and one slip of the foot means that you will plunge

48

from this world into the next. The most stalwart Highlander divests himself of every burden to go round that awful corner."

Later Mr Greg told his own story and pointed out that the Bad Step was not nearly so fearsome as the *Telegraph* suggested, that the holds were ample and that it was only fifteen feet above the sea. From the head of Loch Coruisk he made for the pass between Bidein Druim nan Ramh and Sgurr a' Mhadaidh, but, in mist and rain, gained the ridge to the south of it. Darkness was rapidly coming on as he descended on the Glen Brittle side. When well down he slipped and fell about thirty feet on to scree, receiving bruises and strains but no serious injury. He spent the night where he fell and started again at daybreak, making very slow progress because of his injuries. He crossed the River Brittle but failed to find the path to Sligachan, so spent another night out, this time on heather. On the third morning he reached the road from Carbost to Glen Brittle, so just lay down and slept, knowing someone would be sure to find him. As he was out for forty-seven hours in stormy weather it was a remarkable feat of endurance. The papers made much of it, gave stern warnings as to solitary wanderings in the Cuillin and stressed the need for guides. (No. 19.)

The magazine writers also spread the fame of Skye. About this time the *Graphic, The Field* and the *Cornhill Magazine* all had articles about climbing in the Cuillin. The number of visitors increased; John was busier than ever. When first asked to take a lady up the Pinnacle Ridge of Sgurr nan Gillean he hesitated, and only agreed when a climber whom he knew joined the party. If we judge by the *Graphic's* illustration of an experienced woman climber at Sligachan in 1898, we may well understand John's hesitation, wonder, too, how such a costume would stand up to the rough adhesive gabbro of the Cuillin.

Climbing was still a stately game. One tourist pondered long over the problem of the kind of drink to take with him, then, remembering a friend's advice that Swiss guides always preferred a red wine, made that his choice. The majority, however, preferred Talisker and John's chief worry was to deliver the bottles safely at the top of the climb.

During the last ten years of the ninteenth century the Victorian age was at its zenith. Private steam yachts became very common in West Highland seas. Portree was always a port of call, with a few days at Sligachan almost a ritual. There is but little evidence of yachting parties doing much climbing, though doubtless John Mackenzie took more than one of them up Sgurr nan Gillean.

John Mackenzie climbed among the Cuillin for over fifty years. Thousands of climbers had their introduction to the peaks under his guidance and he took part in innumerable first ascents. During that long period there is no record of any party for which he was responsible being involved in an accident. Never was John lost in the Cuillin; never did he fail to bring his clients safely home again. Often he had to nurse up novices who knew nothing of the sport; often to lead critical experts on the hardest of climbs. All sang his praises.

WOMAN CLIMBER IN SKYE
(from *The Graphic*, 1898)

It is doubtful if anyone will ever have the unique knowledge of the Cuillin which was John's. Every peak and pinnacle was known to him, every corrie and lochan. He was a fount of knowledge in the matter of place-names; the ways of all wild things of the mountain were as an open book to him. He was a wily fisherman and knew well the rivers and lochs of Skye.

John was much more than a guide, he was the best of companions. Often the experts took John with them, not because they really required his services as a guide, but because his company made the expedition so much the more memorable. Gaelic was his mother tongue and he was well on in life before he had a full command of English. In 1895 A. P. Abraham's party made the ascent of the Inaccessible Pinnacle, by the steeper western side, at that time considered something of a feat. When they returned to Sligachan they told John about it.

"What?" said he. "By the short side? But it is impossible."

"Excuse me," said one of the climbers, "but I said we had climbed it."

"Yes, sir," returned John, "I don't doubt your word, only I know it's impossible; I've been up it ma'sel!"

John's English was not too good then, and he was construing "extremely difficult" and "impossible" as one and the same thing.

Had John kept a "Guide's Book", as they do in the Alps, what a story it would have told. The only records lie now in the countless references to him in the Climbers' Book at Sligachan and in the memories of those still living who knew him in his later years. The overwhelming memory is of his kindness and geniality and his own intense pleasure in the mountain scene.

Sheriff Valentine has given us the best picture of the man:

"Of all the pioneers he was the trusty and faithful friend, of others less ambitious the guardian and mentor.

"His independence he always retained. He had his croft and could live without the tourist. In later life he went only occasionally to the mountains, but gave most of the summer to his old and constant ally, Collie. His was a green and sturdy eld. His stride was long and his eye keen. When his companions, wearied by a hard day, had sat themselves down with relief, they would see him set forth in the dusk for the three miles trudge to his cottage, as fresh as a youth in his prime and that when he was already far on in the sixties. The stalker's cap, the loose jacket and knickerbockers which he wore suited the man; they seemed to grow out of him.

"He had the characteristics of the Highlander; the courtesy joined to self-respect that are the heritage of the clans. His accent to the end smacked something of the Gaelic speaker and the turns of his phrases showed in what language his thoughts has been moulded. His features were strong and embrowned by weather. He wore in the old style a short beard, whiskers and moustache. Always alert, always cheerful he was a perfect companion, but it was when the mist came down on the wet rocks that his worth was known. Scottish cragsmen may be content and proud to have him as a leader and a memory."

And what says Collie, that old and trusty ally?

"He is the only real British Climbing Guide that has ever existed. Neither the Lake District nor North Wales has produced one. His great love of the mountains, his keen pleasure in all the beauties of the Cuillin never fails; whether it is a distant view of the mountains, or a sunset fading away behind the Outer Hebrides or the great slabs of gabbro bending over into space, or a still pool of clear water reflecting the rowan bushes and the peaks beyond, or the autumn colour on the rolling moors backed by the hills and the sea—all these do not pass him by unnoticed. He understands not only the joy of a hard climb but can also appreciate the marvels a beautiful mountain land is perpetually offering to one."

To appreciate Collie's tribute one must understand Collie's unique place in world mountaineering.

Three years younger than John Mackenzie, he was born in Manchester, though of Scottish blood. A brilliant student, he took his degree in chemistry in 1884, and after acting as lecturer and demonstrator became Professor of Organic Chemistry at University College, London, and finally succeeded to the post of Director of Chemical Laboratories. Many famous scientists received their training from him and owed much to his inspiration. Widely acknowledged as a successful teacher, he became a Fellow of the Royal Society, while the Universities of Glasgow and St Andrews honoured him with the degree of LL.D. and Liverpool conferred the degree of D.Sc. upon him.

In 1886 Collie came to Sligachan to fish. The weather was fine, the fishing poor, so he started to explore the hills instead. One day in Coir' a' Bhasteir he saw two mountaineers. These were Messrs Stocker and Parker, who were then making a new climb on the fourth pinnacle of Sgurr nan Gillean and who had previously made the first ascent of the short western ridge of the Inaccessible.

"Hundreds of feet above me, on what appeared to me to be rocks as steep as the walls of a house, they moved slowly backwards and forwards, but always getting higher, till they finally reached the summit. I knew nothing about climbing, and it seemed to me perfectly marvellous that human beings should be able to do such things."

52

That evening he got as much information as he could from them, and when told that a rope was necessary for safety in rock climbing, at once telegraphed to London for one. When it arrived Collie and his brother went straight off up the Basteir corrie, but the narrow west ridge was too much for them and they gave up the attempt. On the next day they tried the Pinnacle Ridge and were again defeated, so had to seek out John Mackenzie and ask his advice. John pointed out the tourist route to the summit and by this route they gained the peak at their third attempt.

Such was Collie's introduction to mountaineering. For the next twenty-five years mountaineering became more important to him than fishing, became, for him, an enduring passion.

The Cuillin had captured Collie. Every other summer thereafter he returned. By 1888 he had ascended all the main peaks, invariably with John Mackenzie as his companion. His longest expedition was on the last day of his holidays in 1888. John and he started from Sligachan, ascended by Coire na Creiche to Bealach na Glaic Moire, then traversed all the peaks of Sgurr a' Mhadaidh, Sgurr a' Ghreadaidh and Sgurr na Banachdich to the Inaccessible Pinnacle. A very strong wind made things difficult, but John refused to be beaten, took off his boots and led up the steep west side, the fifth ascent by this side and the fourth in which John had taken part. So difficult were the conditions that Collie admits he went up on the rope. With the Pilkingtons, John had been the follower; with Collie he was, as often as not, the leader.

Collie and John then followed Hart's route over the peaks around Coire Lagan. Like Hart they were stopped by the precipice on the south face of Sgurr Mhic Coinnich, so retreated and found a traverse by a ledge on the Coire Lagan face, which is now known as Collie's Ledge. Collie had a barometer with him and he was the first to point out that Sgurr Alasdair was actually the highest point of the Cuillin and not Sgurr Dearg, as thought by the map-makers of that time.

It was September and the sun was already setting. The easy way home was by the Stone Shoot and Glen Brittle, too easy for such a pair. Instead, they followed the Pilkington route towards Sgurr Dubh and like them were stopped by the great gap on the ridge between Sgurr Thearlaich and Sgurr Dubh. That meant a retreat right back to Sgurr Alasdair and beyond, then a long scree traverse to Bealach Coir' an Lochain and down that interminable corrie towards Coruisk, arriving at the river just as the last blink of sunset was fading. Collie never forgot the impressions he received that night—the gloom and the grandeur and the sense of being cut off from all the world. They took the direct route over Druim nan Ramh, which involved fifteen hundred feet of steep climbing, found their way down Harta Corrie by starlight, then floundered along the Sligachan glen to reach the hotel at midnight.

In 1918 at the end of his climbing career, which had taken him to all the great mountain ranges of the world, Collie described that expedition in the Cuillin as "one of the hardest of them all".

By 1890 Collie was attempting Alpine peaks, together with Hastings and Mummery, the party being described as one of the finest that ever climbed in the Alps. Many notable first ascents were theirs. 1895 found them in the Himalaya, and Collie has told us the story of it in that grand book, *Climbing on the Himalaya and other Mountain Ranges.* An expedition to the Lofoten Isles yielded more first ascents, and was followed by various expeditions to the Rocky Mountains of Canada, where many virgin peaks fell to his party.

"A leader of inspired direction", his fame became world-wide. Within a short time after its formation he became a member of the Scottish Mountaineering Club and was later made an Honorary Member. He also became President of the Alpine Club and Chairman of the Mount Everest Committee.

Always in the seasons when he was not climbing in other countries he returned to Skye, and John Mackenzie became his inseparable companion.

He set himself the task of measuring accurately the height of every single peak of the Cuillin and of the passes between them. At first he had some difficulty; on two separate days, after having carefully set the aneroid before starting in the morning, on his return in the evening the whole of Sligachan Inn was found according to the aneroid, on one occasion below sea-level, while on the next it appeared to be at a height of over one hundred feet!

Collie therefore adopted the method of setting the aneroid by an already observed Ordnance Survey point in the Cuillin which he took to be correct and then moving as rapidly as possible along the ridge, noting the reading at places omitted from the Ordnance Map till he reached their next station. By this method ascent and descent were small, never more than 300–500 feet, so reducing to the minimum a possible source of error—changing atmospheric pressure.

Readings were checked and rechecked by other climbers, who were thus of great help to the Ordnance Survey.

It was on his return from the Himalaya in 1896 that he first started to attack the rock faces of the Cuillin, then almost untouched, and often he wrote of the ascent of the Coruisk face of Sgurr a' Ghreadaidh which gives almost two thousand feet of climbing on bare rock: (No. 13)

> "There the climber will see the bare grey rocks rising out of the heather not 500 feet above the level of the loch; and the walls, ridges and towers of weather-worn gabbro stretch with hardly a break to the summit of the mountain. He must climb up gullies that the mountain torrents have worn out of the precipices and over slabs of rock sloping down into space at an angle that makes handhold necessary; he must creep out round edges on the face of the perpendicular cliffs, only to find that, after all, the perpendicular cliff itself must be scaled before he can win back to the ridge that is to lead him to the topmost peak."

It was the same summer that he did the first face climb of Sgurr Alasdair, the Thearlaich-Dubh gap which had defeated him in 1888 having been conquered in 1891. Other routes where his party was the first to tread include the gully between the third and fourth pinnacle of Sgurr nan Gillean, the Basteir Tooth from Lota Corrie, the Window Buttress of Sgurr Dearg, Sgurr Coir' an Lochain and Sron na Ciche.

Of all his new ways in Skye the discovery of Sron na Ciche might well be termed the most important. In 1899 Major Bruce (later General Bruce and well-known for his exploits in the Himalaya) came to Skye with his Gurkha, Harkabir Thapa, and the Gurkha has left his name in the annals of Skye climbing, for he ascended Glamaig (2,537 feet) from Sligachan in thirty-seven minutes and descended in eighteen minutes. Though there have been several attempts no one has ever succeeded in beating that record, nor is it likely anyone will ever do so. The normal climber takes about an hour and a half to plug up the scree slopes of Glamaig.

Collie did much climbing with Bruce and Harkabir Thapa. On one occasion they were on Sgurr Alasdair and were much delayed while returning in upper Coire Lagan by rescuing crag-bound sheep. When they reached the lochan the sun was already low down, throwing heavy shadows across the cliffs on the south side of the lower corrie. Collie at once noticed a great shadow about the middle of the cliffs and deduced that it must be thrown by a huge rock tower standing out from the cliffs. He photographed it and the result was much the same as my own photograph (No. 32), which was also taken in the evening.

An investigation was indicated, but, curiously, it was not until 1906 that Collie again sought these cliffs. To us today such delay seems very strange, but we are accustomed to reach Sron na Ciche within an hour from hotel, hostel or camp in Glen Brittle. Fifty years ago the only accommodation was at Sligachan, and climbers usually descended by Coire Lagan late in the day with a long trek to Sligachan before them. Those who took Coire Lagan on their way to the hills were intent on higher peaks, while the position of the sun would not cause such a shadow early in the day.

In 1906 Collie and his friend Colin Phillip got the use of the Shooting Lodge at Glen Brittle. This made for much easier access. On the very first day Collie went up to Coire Lagan to find out what kind of rock cast the shadow. He soon saw that it was real enough, realised too that the great precipice might well provide dozens of routes for the cragsman. Collie tried to reach the jutting-out crag but made little headway and decided to wait till John Mackenzie was with him. Collie describes it:

> "From top of the precipice to the bottom is at least a thousand feet, perpendicular in many places and a narrow knife edge of rock about a hundred feet long runs out from it rather less than halfway down. On each side of the knife edge are steep clean slabs of rock that, at their base, overhang the gullies below. At the end of the knife edge is placed the tower which casts its shadow across the great slab."

Its name, A' Chioch (the Pap), was an inspiration of John Mackenzie on the first ascent. Let Collie continue the story:

> "The climb was full of excitement for one never knew what was round the next corner. We traversed slabs, we worked up cracks and went right away from the Cioch, into the gully on the east side of it, losing sight of it altogether. Then we fortunately found a queer traverse that led out of the gully across the perpendicular face of the cliff and back in the direction of the Cioch. But the Cioch itself we could not see until having got round several corners suddenly it came into view and we found ourselves on the end of the knife edge. We slowly made our way to the great tower at its end up which we climbed." (Nos. 25, 27.)

John Mackenzie led the way, his being the first foot to touch that queer rock now so often called the Mecca of British cragsmen. Collie was delighted and introduced all other members of his own party to the Cioch during the following month. John and he also discovered many other routes on Sron na Ciche and thus opened up an entirely new phase of Skye climbing.

The Climbers Arrive

Collie climbed with many of the pioneers, but his greatest friend was Colin Phillip, more a painter than a climber, with whom he shared the tenancy of Glen Brittle Lodge for many summers from 1906 onwards. As the years passed by Collie lengthened his holidays in Skye, usually arriving in mid-July and leaving in mid-September. When he retired from his work in 1929 his summer at Sligachan extended from spring till well into autumn. By then he was too old to climb and John was ever his companion on his fishing exploits.

John Mackenzie died in 1934. Collie was deeply affected, for they had been companions for fifty years—indeed John was almost his other self. Collie was never quite the same afterwards, his obituary of John, which has already been quoted, telling something of his feelings. Almost all of Collie's climbing contemporaries were dead, and he himself was almost a legendary figure—one of the few surviving links with the golden age of climbing. By some Collie was thought rather intolerant, for he did not take to strangers readily and did not suffer fools gladly. An incident of his early days gives a revealing picture of the man. With two men he was on the Ennerdale face of the Pillar Rock in Lakeland when his leader fell from the difficult hand traverse, the whole party being lucky to escape without serious injury. Some time afterwards he was there again with another party. One of them insisted on trying the hand traverse. Collie said he had seen one leader fall from it and did not wish to repeat the experience. The man still insisted, so Collie said: "If we are roped, I shall prevent your starting; if we are not, I shall go down at once." The man still protested, but, adds Collie, he did not attempt the traverse.

At Sligachan latterly he had his favourite chair in the outer vestibule, and there he sat looking out to Glamaig with a far-away look in his eyes, enveloped in smoke and memories. Only to a small circle of his intimates did he unbend. To them he talked freely and with great knowledge and authority, but usually the talk veered round to his early climbing days and his exploits with John Mackenzie.

Some of the finest articles which have appeared in mountaineering club journals were from Collie's pen. He detested that type of article which gave times and distances like a railway time-table and failed to appreciate the wondrous beauty of the mountain scene. His own water-colours show the hand of the gifted artist. To a great age he remained erect, hardy and agile and retained his interest in the mountains till the very end. In 1938, when in his eightieth year, he made the long journey from London to attend the Jubilee

57

Dinner of the Cairngorm Club at Aberdeen, of which club he was the Honorary President.

When war came in 1939 he remained at Sligachan. All guests departed from the hotel. Access to Skye was difficult; he was alone. He continued to fish, but gradually grew frailer. It was fitting that the last glimpse given to us of the old mountaineer should have been by the eager young man who gave his life in the Battle of Britain. Collie lingered on. When the end was near several friends tried to reach him. Only one, Mr Lee, managed to get to Skye and was with him when he died on November 1st, 1942, at the age of eighty-three.

THE SCOTTISH MOUNTAINEERING CLUB

The Alpine Club was formed in 1857, the Swiss Alpine Club in 1863 and the French Alpine Club in 1874. On January 10th, 1889, there appeared in the *Glasgow Herald* a letter from Mr W. W. Naismith headed "Proposal for a Scottish Alpine Club". In it he described mountain climbing, "one of the most manly as well as healthful and fascinating forms of exercise", and declared that it was "almost a disgrace that any Scotsman whose heart and lungs are in proper order if he is not more or less of a mountaineer seeing that he belongs to one of the most mountainous countries in the world", and ended by suggesting that a Scottish Alpine Club be formed. Other letters followed and on February 11th of that year the Scottish Mountaineering Club had its birth.

The Alpine Club gave full support, fourteen of its members being among the original hundred members, including Clinton Dent, then its president, and Charles and Lawrence Pilkington. For the rest of his life Naismith, "a human being of the finest steel, modest and self-effacing", was known as the much loved father of the S.M.C.

At that time the mountains of Scotland had never been classified. No one knew the exact number over three thousand feet high, and many were unknown, unclimbed, unmeasured. The first job to be done was therefore the compilation of an accurate list of names and heights.

Mr Hugh Munro (later Sir Hugh) undertook this monumental task and ensured undying fame, for the name "Munro" applied to a Scottish mountain over three thousand feet high has passed into the language. Munro worked hard and by the end of 1891 the *S.M.C. Journal* published his tables of 538 tops over three thousand feet, of which 283 were judged to be separate mountains and the remainder subsidiary tops (the latest revised list gives 543 and 276).

This list showed nine "Munros" in Skye and three other tops, and it is noticeable that heights were given from Dr Collie's notes, these being reckoned much more accurate than the Ordnance Survey figures. The O.S. map was shown to be most misleading and climbers preferred that prepared by Charles Pilkington.

The S.M.C. at once started to attack the Skye peaks. Apart from the Alpine Club men, only Naismith had experience of climbing in Skye before the club's formation. In 1880 he climbed Blaven, Bruach na Frithe, Sgurr nan Gillean and made the first ascent of the northern peak of Bidein Druim nan Ramh, though, because of the inaccurate map of that time, he thought he was on the north peak of Sgurr a' Mhadaidh.

After the formation of the club Naismith teamed up with other pioneers, both English and Scottish, and took part usually as leader in many first ascents all over Scotland, as mountaineering guide-books testify to this day, and of course he introduced many fellow members to the Cuillin. He was the first to give a complete and accurate description of the Pinnacle Ridge of Sgurr nan Gillean, now a classic among British rock climbs. When he and William Douglas first viewed the fearsome "gendarme" on the west ridge of Sgurr nan Gillean one stormy evening they very much doubted if it would "go". So they adopted a plan which often succeeded—"camped in full view of the difficulty, discussed it leisurely, smoked a pipe over it, made fun of it and finally strolled across without much difficulty". (Nos. 18, 63.)

1892 saw the first Easter climbing party at Sligachan—J. H. Wicks, G. H. Morse, Ellis Carr, J. H. Gibson—and the first to have experience of climbing the Cuillin in snow, their opinion being that under such conditions the Cuillin may be more fitly compared with the Alps than the Central Highlands with the Cuillin.

With several days at Sligachan, two nights at Glen Brittle farmhouse and one night's camp at Coruisk they managed to cover the greater part of the main ridge. This is the first record of climbers who camped out in the Cuillin. The Alpine tradition that porters be engaged to carry all equipment held good for many years in Skye. Thus the party were able to traverse Sgurr Sgumain, Sgurr Alasdair and Sgurr Mhic Coinnich unburdened, then descend to Coruisk, where at a prearranged spot, tent, blankets and provisions lay awaiting them, having been brought over from Sligachan on pony-back by a ghillie. They used a three-man Whymper tent and a one-man Mummery tent and had a very comforting meal of Irish stew, coffee, cold beef, tinned peaches and whisky. Before they had finished breakfast in the morning the ghillie had returned with the pony to collect all equipment, leaving the party free for another spell of ridge walking.

The climber of today must be his own beast of burden and a remote camp means usually two days less for climbing. The early climbers had great difficulty because of the inaccuracy of the Ordnance Survey one-inch map of the Cuillin; so much so that Collie claimed the map had problems more difficult to solve than the ascent of many of the peaks. The first map based on modern methods of survey was the Admiralty effort mentioned by C. R. Weld. It named only some of the South Cuillin as seen from Loch Scavaig and left blank the entire northern part of the range. The Ordnance Survey one-inch map first appeared in 1885; as Sgurr Dearg was the only peak of the seven highest which the surveyors managed to climb, and as they only measured eleven out of thirty-three tops, making the links between them with the eye of faith and making contour lines run through ridges, it is small wonder that climbers were confused.

Something had to be done about that map. The S.M.C. had many influential members. Did not one of them, a sheriff, proudly proclaim at a meeting: "Fannich is mine, I have full civil and criminal jurisdiction in Mullach Coire Mhic Fhearchair, and even over the corrie of Meall a' Chinn Dearg which has recently been translated as the bald hill with the red head", and go on to talk of the other sporting corners of his jurisdiction and assure his hearers that he had accepted the appointment mainly that the objects of Scottish mountaineering be furthered and that the interest of property and the law of the land would weigh as nothing against the legitimate claims of their sport?

Sir Archibald Geikie was another famous member. The complaints about the poor maps reached his ear and he it was who, in 1895, suggested that Dr Alfred Harker be appointed to the Geological Survey of Scotland for special fieldwork in the Cuillin of Skye. For six years Harker devoted himself to the difficult and complicated job of mapping the Cuillin. Mostly he worked from Sligachan but now and then from Glen Brittle, and once he camped by Loch Scavaig with John Mackenzie as his helper. Every peak, every corrie, every ridge of the Cuillin was known to him, yet he did not call himself a rock climber and never climbed on a rope.

The *S.M.C. Journal* of 1897 had a list of all the Cuillin peaks and heights. Harker corrected and made many additions to this list, and by 1898 the club had reprinted a map of the Cuillin on which Harker marked in red all his

38. Am Basteir and Basteir Tooth. Between the two is King's Cave Chimney, first climbed by King's party in 1898. Slanting up to the right of it is Shadbolt's Chimney, first climbed by Shadbolt and MacLaren in 1906. Naismith's original route is on the far side of the Tooth

main routes and important ways. From that time to this Harker's map has been the guide and the saviour of generations of climbers.

Still the development was entirely by way of ridge walking. This period lasted for approximately thirty years, from Nicolson's first wanderings in 1865 till 1895. That year marked the epic assault on the Waterpipe Gully which is mentioned in the next chapter. Thus was started a new era of climbing in Skye, the following few years being years of great achievement.

In 1896 the S.M.C. were in force at Sligachan: Collie, Naismith, Phillip, Dr Collier, Howell, Parker, Douglas, Rennie with George Sang and Dr Inglis Clark making a first visit. The campaign was opened in June, when Rennie and Douglas sailed a yacht into Loch Scavaig and had fine climbing on the ridges of the Dubhs.

Dr Inglis Clark later became the most efficient of S.M.C. secretaries and the one who first made the arranging of a mountaineering meet into something of a fine art. He was on his first visit to Skye. Up till then his climbing had been almost entirely hill walking, so making his Skye achievements the more notable. These included Sgurr nan Gillean by Pinnacle and West Ridge, Am Basteir and its Tooth and Clach Glas and Blaven.

All during July and August parties were on the ridges, but it was not till September that new climbs were attempted. Even today the face climbs done that month are among the most notable in Skye. On the very first day of the month Collie led Howell on the now famous long climb of Sgurr a' Ghreadaidh —two thousand feet on first-rate bare rocks. On the 3rd the same two with Naismith and Phillip made a frontal attack on Sgurr Alasdair from Coire Lagan —a thousand feet of magnificent climbing. On the 4th Naismith and Parker climbed Sgurr na h-Uamha by its south face from Harta Corrie, descended to Lota Corrie and made short new climbs from there to the summit of Sgurr a' Fhionn Choire.

Next day, joining up with Howell and Collie, the great north-west buttress of Sgurr a' Mhadaidh was conquered. Other first ascents were on the west face of Clach Glas and the gully between the second and third pinnacles of Sgurr nan Gillean.

Finally and fittingly Collie, Howell, Naismith and John Mackenzie from a camp beside Loch Coruisk made the first ascent of Sgurr Coir' an Lochain. This peak juts out from the main ridge, from which it is separated by a deep gap. The last Cuillin peak had capitulated. Sixty years had elapsed since Professor Forbes led the way.

The club was in something of a glow after all these first ascents and great things were planned for 1897. Sligachan was all very well but too far away from the southern part of the range where there was still so much exploring to be done. Why not follow Douglas's idea and have a floating base in Loch Scavaig? (No. 55.)

So it came about that a yachting meet was arranged for Easter 1897, the main party (thirteen in all) joining at Oban. Seas ran high. The rounding of Ardnamurchan Point damped the ardour of a goodly number, though spirits revived when the yacht anchored in Loch Scavaig under the very shadow of the Cuillin. To remain was impossible, for Loch Scavaig with a south-west gale blowing into it offered neither comfort nor security. The anchorage at the Isle of Soay was then tried, but under the conditions it was not considered safe. Finally a retreat had to be made to the more sheltered anchorage at Loch Scresort in Rhum. Stormy weather preventing an immediate return to Loch Scavaig, the yacht made for Loch Hourn, the idea being that some peaks be climbed from there, while it was near enough to make a return to Skye possible should the weather improve. The weather did not improve and the party never set foot in Skye. W. N. Ling attended that historic meet, and in 1950 attended his hundreth meet at Corrie.

Douglas, Rennie, Brown and Barrow were also on board and determined they *would* have a climbing base for the south Cuillin and not unnaturally, after such an experience, decided that it must be on land. They did not think a tent would stand up to the rigours of Skye weather, hence they conceived the idea of a portable house or, in the language of today, a prefab! Alfred Williams and other artists had previously used such huts at Coruisk and their experience was of value. Finally Rennie designed a structure of wood and felt. Tent-shaped, the base of the two triangles was $9\frac{1}{2}$ feet and the height 8 feet, which allowed for a wooden door 4 feet 9 inches by 2 feet at one end. The sides were 8 feet long, consisting of a ridge-pole, seven horizontal and two vertical spars. The wood was bought from a joiner and all cut up by the party themselves. For three huts there were 110 lengths of wood of varying lengths and 2 inches to 6 inches broad, plus some planking for the floor; 25 yards of roofing-felt formed the covering. The cost of the material for each hut was 26s.; today the odd planks for the flooring of one of them might well cost more than that. (No. 29.)

The two sleeping-huts were lined with thin white cloth and furnished with two camp-beds each. The third or cookhouse had an extension at the back to accommodate coke and primus stoves and was furnished with a folding table and four chairs.

The list of provisions must remind the climber of the supplies Albert Smith took with him on his ascent of Mont Blanc, even though the Scottish party do not seem to have followed Alfred William's example of laying on a cache of beer. Our four hoped to be at Coruisk for about a month, and provisioned themselves thus:

24 2-lb. tins soup	7 lb. ships' biscuits
14 2-lb. tins meat	2 boxes ginger nuts
4 tins tomatoes	12 2-lb. jars jam
2 tins pears	12 tins condensed milk
4 lb. dried apples	3 tins sardines
4 lb. dried apricots	3 tins Maggi soap
5 lb. prunes	2 lb. flour
2 lb. figs.	4 lb. lard
7 lb. rice	3 lb. macaroni
14 lb. oatmeal	14 lb. ham
2 lb. coffee	4 dozen eggs
3 lb. tea	8 lb. butter
$\frac{1}{4}$ lb. cocoa	1 stone potatoes
14 lb. sugar	6 lb. onions
5 lb. cheese	12 dozen oranges
7 lb. beans	12 2-lb. loaves
7 lb. wheaten biscuits	mustard, pepper, salt, pickles, sauces

They had to renew their supply of oatmeal, sugar, milk, butter, rice and bread from the weekly steamer and were also able to obtain eggs and milk from Camasunary and fish from Soay.

Those of us who had to solve the problem of supplying food for even one week's camp in Skye in immediate post-war years, when even bread was rationed and neither fish nor eggs could be obtained, may sigh for these good old days.

The Coruisk campers also took 2 gallons of tar, 4 gallons of paraffin oil, 2 cwt. of coke, spades, hammers, saws, lanterns and 14 lb. of nails and screws with which to join up the huts.

On July 20th MacBrayne's steamer, *The Gael*, landed them and all their impedimenta at Loch Scavaig. A rowing-boat had previously been carried up to Loch Coruisk by Soay fishermen, three of whom met the climbers and assisted in the rough half-mile of porterage from Scavaig to Coruisk. From there to the head of Coruisk is two miles and it took seven journeys to transport all the baggage. By nightfall two of the huts were erected.

While the site of the camp—that oasis of greenery by the river at the head of the loch—is a most picturesque one, it is not perfect, as it rapidly becomes a bog in wet weather. A better site could have been found at the south end of the loch which would also have avoided much of the porterage, but the party preferred privacy and did not wish to be overrun with trippers once a week when they landed from the tourist steamer. (Nos. 30, 31.)

That day was dry, as were the next two, which were spent in erecting the cookhouse and getting the entire camp into working order. In that they were lucky: a good many climbers have had several holidays in Skye without experiencing three successive dry days.

Then came a week of rain, a week of dry weather (more or less), though very sultry, a week of storms finishing up with a day or two of sunshine. The first stormy night gave alarm till they knew the fabric of the hut would stand up to it; they soon realised why this place is called the "water cauldron". In front of the camp was the loch with its little islands stretching to Sgurr na Stri which blocked the view in that direction. On either side steep slabby rocks rose up to the summit of Sgurr Dubh and Druim nan Ramh, while behind the camp circled the main Cuillin range. The valley formed something of a funnel; the wind roared through it and when the heavens opened it became a very cauldron of fury.

A flooded river once carried their boat away and returned it upside down, while the loch, suddenly rising, stole a bag of coke and a drum of tar which they had left at the water's edge. One night the storm was such that they slept in their clothes. All night long the rain came down in torrents, the river rose in flood and ran racing past within a few feet of the huts. The smooth slabby sides of Sgurr Dubh were converted into one vast waterslide and the water cascaded down, threatening to flood out the entire camp, the wind howling fiendishly the while.

Many nights were like that. It was indeed the stormiest weather for many years; at Sligachan the river was higher than ever previously recorded, while Sgurr nan Gillean was struck by lightning, the topmost slab being split in two.

Nevertheless much good climbing was done. All parts of the ridge were visited at one time or the other and the Thearlaich-Dubh gap was traversed three times. Collie's long climb on Sgurr a' Ghreadaidh was repeated, while they made a notable first ascent of the south-east buttress of the Coir' Uaigneis face of Sgurr a' Mhadaidh.

On many occasions they carried with them quarter-plate, half-plate and whole-plate cameras. While climbers would rejoice were such pre-fabs available at Loch Coruisk today, they would shudder at the thought of lugging forty pounds of photographic apparatus on their climbs. William Douglas was the photographer of the party and set the high standard which has characterised serious S.M.C. photographers to this day. All agreed that easily reached Sgurr na Stri was by far the finest stance for a comprehensive view of the Cuillin.

Since that time no one has ever had such a long camp at Coruisk and even we who know the area so well may not fully realise just what it means

> "to live for five weeks in the heart of Coruisk; to see Sgurr a' Ghreadaidh slowly forming out of the gloom of the morning mists; to see, when some storm had passed, the wet slabs of the Cuillin glistening in sunlight; to see, when the sun had set, shafts of light darting through every cleft in the Banachdich ridge and thrusting golden streamers into the darkness of the corries and to feel continually the near presence of the immense black peaks that crowded the lonely camp."

1897 also was the year of his first visit to Skye by Harold Raeburn, that bold and resolute leader who was to leave his name so strongly imprinted on both Scottish and world mountaineering. He visited the party at Coruisk several times; usually a thunderstorm greeted him. Nevertheless he took part in some of their climbs and also did much climbing from Sligachan. Though his introduction to the Cuillin was a very stormy one, he was back most seasons thereafter, one of his first efforts in 1898 being to force a way up the Basteir ravine without having a bath like the A.C. party of 1890.

In 1898 Dr and Mrs Inglis Clark, James Parker and A. E. Robertson opened the campaign in June. Most of the now classic routes were followed, while Robertson towards the end of the month climbed Sgurr na Banachdich alone, the seventy-fifth mountain over three thousand feet high he had climbed since April 1st. Here surely is a prince of peak-baggers. In the years previous to that he had ascended a hundred Munros and his feat of 1898 set him well on his way to climbing the whole 283, a task he duly accomplished in September 1901. Only a dozen climbers have done so since then.

The Cuillin of Skye

The strong party gathered at Sligachan in August 1898 had good weather and were on the hills almost every day. Though every peak in the Cuillin had been climbed by 1895, the entire crest of the main ridge had not been followed in two places. Actually there are four difficult parts on the ridge, the Inaccessible, the Thearlaich-Dubh gap, the ascent from the col between Sgurr Thearlaich and Sgurr Mhic Coinnich to the summit of the latter peak and a direct ascent of the Basteir Tooth. Very fittingly three of the main pioneers were involved in the solving of these last three problems. Collie with W. W. King and John Mackenzie crossed the famous gap for the first time in 1891. W. W. King, Naismith and Douglas made the first ascent of King's Chimney of Mhic Coinnich in 1898, and in the same year Naismith and A. M. Mackay "bagged the last portion of the main ridge which required straightening out". All three climbs are now included in the main ridge traverse, though the gap was once declared "impracticable" by a President of the Alpine Club, and the overhang of the Tooth daunted even Collie. (Nos. 35, 36, 37.)

As these three, together with the "Inaccessible", are the tit-bits of the ridge some description is necessary. If one approaches the gap for the first time on a wet misty day one can well believe how impossible it seemed to the pioneers. It is an abrupt cleft on a very narrow part of the ridge, where if approaching from the south the wall falls away absolutely vertically for twenty-five feet to the gap, then rises almost vertically for about eighty feet. Very often the last man has to use a doubled rope when descending the short side, while the way up the longer side is by the narrow crack which shows up so well in the photograph. The guide-book modestly puts it: "As the passage is not easy, all members of the party should not descend into the gap at one time in case they may have to remain there permanently." (No. 36.)

Collie on gaining the summit of Sgurr Mhic Coinnich had descended and followed a ledge on the Coire Lagan side to the col, but King led direct upwards from the col by a well-marked chimney which is blocked by an overhang near the top, causing a traverse on the right on rather small holds, then upwards to the summit. (No. 35.)

Am Basteir with its Tooth is a great feature of the Sligachan end of the ridge. Approaching the Tooth from the south, Collie descended well into Lota Corrie, then climbed up to the gap between Tooth and peak from where the top of the Tooth is easily reached. Naismith also reached its top by this route, then he prospected the overhang at the end of a rope and decided that it could be climbed direct from below. This he did, his companion (now Lord Mackay) describing it as an act of faith and telling how at the steepest part he himself detached a piece of rock which dropped clear for three hundred feet before it touched the screes below. All who make the traverse note the great exposure and sensational outlook, adequate and sound holds making it a normal course. (No. 37.)

The entire main ridge by its crest had now been conquered and more intensive exploration was called for. King led Naismith up the Basteir face of the fourth pinnacle of Sgurr nan Gillean, then Naismith led J. F. Dobson and A. M. Mackay up the Forked Chimney of the Main Peak. King then decided it was time for a new route up the Inaccessible Pinnacle. This was on the precipitous south face by a crack which he had noted previously. From the screes below this looks very formidable and the pioneers wisely decided that the safety of a rope from above was essential for its initial exploration. Two of them climbed the pinnacle by its easy east side and let down a rope to King, who had patiently waited below. So safeguarded, King made the ascent, noting an awkward section about thirty feet up where a bulge forces the climber out of the crack. The standard of exposure was such that no one tried it during the eight years which followed.

But the most interesting new climb of 1898 was undoubtedly the ascent of King's Cave Chimney of Am Basteir. It seems that long ago the nick between the Tooth and Am Basteir was much deeper than at present and that in course of time it became jammed up with debris and boulders. This has led to the formation of caves between the boulders and at different levels, the gully being described as having a basement, first, second and third floors, together with a window halfway up. (No. 38.)

Exploration took the greater part of four days. On the first day Naismith and King reached the second floor and decided they would have to get a hitch over a certain block at the front of the cave before they could go higher. On the second day most of the time was spent trying to throw a stone at the end of a piece of string over the block so that a rope could later be attached. All attempts failed. On the third day they brought with them a geologist's hammer. With this they enlarged the "window" so that a man could sit on its ledge and from there throw the stone over the forward block.

On the fourth day after all the roping was completed a strong draught of cold air was noted coming from the back of the cave. The leader, King, went to investigate, pushed his head through a hole not much bigger than a rabbit burrow and wriggled on into the darkness till only his boots could be seen.

67

Then he disappeared altogether, till a joyful shout announced his arrival at the top. This route obviated the necessity for all the complicated rope work, but, the way being narrow, will always be a very tight squeeze. One advantage is that, being mostly a subterranean route, it can be done in the wildest weather. Many parties have had difficulty in finding the entrance to the upper funnel and climbers have been known to stick in the narrowest part and to feel they are doomed to remain there for life. Most certainly it is not a place for those of supernormal girth.

A few days later Raeburn and Biggs made the first traverse of the Tooth, ascending by the chimney and descending by Naismith's route.

Every year added to the knowledge of the Cuillin, and 1903 marked the first official meet of any mountaineering club in Skye. Since then, for the S.M.C., as for almost all other British clubs, meets in Skye are among the happiest memories.

Dr Inglis Clark, the secretary, showed his organising genius by booking a saloon carriage for the train journey to Mallaig, and arranging accommodation not only at Sligachan but also at Glen Brittle and Camasunary Lodges. It was Easter and most of the party had never previously seen snow on the Cuillin.

These were the spacious days. The meet lasted for ten days and some of the party had a round tour, staying at each of the three centres. The best effort was that of Raeburn's party, which traversed the Dubhs, the famous gap and Sgurr Thearlaich and Sgurr Alasdair, all under difficult snow conditions.

So enjoyable was that meet that Easter 1905 saw them there again in larger numbers. Ten of those present had been or were yet to be presidents of the club—Rennie, Inglis Clark, Douglas, Ling, Maylard, Munro, Parker, Raeburn, Solly and Walker, while W. Cecil Slingsby showed he had not forgotten Skye after his great exploits in Norway.

Finally in 1907 the 54th issue of the *S.M.C. Journal* was taken up entirely by a complete mountaineer's guide-book to the Isle of Skye. With a bookman such as William Douglas as editor it set a high literary standard, a standard which has not been surpassed by any of the many other guide-books which the club has published since that day. Alas, like most rock-climbing guide-books, it was out of date on publication, as it did not include details of Dr Collie's discovery of the Cioch the previous year, a discovery which was to provide Skye with its finest rock-climbing playground.

About this time arose the controversy as to whether the Cuillin of Skye were the best training ground for the novice rock climber, a controversy which, to

68

some extent, lingers to this day. It all arose through Raeburn telling Inglis Clark that he would not trust a climber who had only climbed in Skye. Inglis Clark thought it almost a profane remark, especially when Raeburn stated that "The Skye climbing as far as my experience goes is ridiculously easy, with the exception of the gap on the Alasdair-Dubh ridge and the lower portions of the rocks near Coruisk." Raeburn later explained his point of view more fully by comparing the nature of climbing on the gabbro of Skye and the granite of Arran.

William Brown, one of the heroes of the Coruisk camp, rushed into print to defend his beloved Cuillin which he held Raeburn had slandered. Brown objected strongly to the estimate of "ridiculously easy" as applied to Skye climbing. He then compared the ridges of Skye with the ridges of Arran, the ridge of Cruachan and other mainland peaks and claimed that the former were much the more difficult. He further maintained that once the main ridge had been left there was literally no end to the difficulties with which a climber might find himself confronted; that Skye rock was not always sound but interspersed with many dangerous and rotten sections. Finally he claimed that Skye was a good centre for the beginner, though qualifying it by the remark that if a climber had not the sense to know he must treat different rocks differently then he ought to give up climbing altogether.

Raeburn, far from capitulating, returned to the attack and gave his reasons much more fully. In Skye the climbs look much more difficult and dangerous than they really are, but when one starts climbing, the rough, hard gabbro affords friction grips in plenty, while the holds are numerous. On the contrary, the granite slabs of the Ben Nuis precipice in Arran seem at no great angle, yet, because of the lack of holds, are difficult and dangerous.

Raeburn then went on to quote Dr Claude Wilson's definition of easy and difficult rock: "Handholds and footholds are spoken of collectively as holds and when these are firm and plentiful the rocks are said to be easy; on 'difficult' rock the holds are scanty or are so small or so awkwardly placed that it requires considerable skill to make use of them."

His final summing up was: "The gabbro of the Cuillin is *too* good, it makes one discontented with one's powers on smoother rocks. It is the very luxury of British climbing, and therefore not the best place for training the novice."

Raeburn's opinion seems to be generally held today, even though climbs of a severity undreamed of by him are now done in Skye.

69

THE ENGLISH CLUBS

The Alpine Club, in its early years, did not consider our British hills a major field for endeavour, looking on them as only fit to provide mild scrambling at weekends and on those occasions on which members could not manage overseas. In Lakeland and Snowdonia rock climbing developed between 1870 and 1890, and, as we have seen, A.C. men found a grand field for exploration in Skye. They could not help but note the great success of the Scottish Mountaineering Club, and A.C. members of that club and other English climbers who had been to Skye played a part in the formation of the chief English clubs.

The first of these, the Yorkshire Ramblers, was formed in 1892, with W. C. Slingsby as President, and Dent, Pilkington and Horace Walker as honorary members, and soon established itself throughout the north of England. Next, in 1898, came the Climbers Club, based on London, but whose spiritual home was Pen-y-Gwryd in Snowdonia. Among original members were Dent, Slingsby and other Skye stalwarts such as W. W. King, R. A. Robertson (then President of the S.M.C.), James Maclay, Harrison Barrow, H. T. Munro and the brothers Abraham, two hundred members joining right at the beginning. Next came the Rucksack Club of Manchester (1902), where S.M.C. were represented by C. Pilkington, Herman Wooley and Howard. Finally the Fell and Rock Climbing Club and the Wayfarers' Club came into being in 1906, the former honouring Collie, Hastings, Pilkington and Solly with honorary membership, while Colin Phillip, Bennet Gibbs, Fred Jackson and Herman Wooley joined the ranks.

From the beginning all these clubs had influential members with experience of climbing in Skye, and these men spread the gospel of the glorious mountaineering possibilities of the Cuillin. All clubs sent their quotas to Sligachan; every year saw an increase in the number of climbers in Skye. For about ten years from its formation S.M.C. members were responsible for working out most of the new climbing routes in Skye. After that, the initiative as regards first ascents gradually passed to the English clubs. After all, the active climbing members of the S.M.C. could be numbered in dozens, those of the English clubs in hundreds, while the S.M.C. were also engaged in exploring great tracts of unknown mountain land on the mainland of Scotland.

Now and then English climbers made a foray to Glencoe or to the Cairngorms, but Skye was ever their main objective. From about 1906 the greatest number of climbers came from south of the border and were responsible for almost all new routes in the Cuillin for the next twenty years. Only when the younger Scottish clubs got into their stride was the balance restored.

It cannot be gainsaid that the general standard of rock climbing in the south was higher than in Scotland during these years. The mountainous areas in Lakeland and Snowdonia are relatively small compared with those of Scotland. They were soon explored and there was concentration on difficult routes, the emphasis always being on rock climbing. In Scotland the emphasis was on snow climbing, as the principal meets of the S.M.C. were held at New Year and Easter.

The pioneers naturally took the easy way to the summit of the unclimbed peaks. Collie led the exploration of the secondary routes by gullies, cracks and chimneys and obvious lines of weakness on the face of the crags. These latter routes in the Cuillin are often indicated by basalt, hence many of Collie's routes have sections of loose rock.

The third stage was when climbers ventured on the more open and steeper faces, which, because of the sound gabbro, yielded many routes.

The most outstanding gully in the Cuillin is that of Sgurr an Fheadain, so it is not surprising that it should have been the first to be explored. Approaching Glen Brittle by road from Carbost, there is one point when the range of the Cuillin bursts suddenly into view; a view which has enthralled generations of climbers. Dominating the scene is the conical peak of Sgurr an Fheadain. It stands out from the others, and right in the centre of its precipitous face is a well-marked gully 1,200 feet in length, its name, the Waterpipe, being an apt description. (No. 39.)

In September 1895 Messrs Kelsall and Hallitt climbed it. True, they made several traverses on the south wall and thus avoided certain pitches in the bed of the gully; even so it was a tremendous achievement when we remember that they did not bother to put on the rope till they were a considerable way up. In their modest account in the Climbers' Book at Sligachan they described the climb as "affording constant, interesting and sometimes difficult climbing". Later climbers described it as without equal in the British Isles, with no less than twenty-five pitches, some of them monstrous. Some indeed were very sceptical about that first ascent, and the following entry appeared in the book:

"As politely as possible (assuming the account to be serious) we desire to protest against the impression left by the description of the gully. It appears to us (and it is putting it mildly) a gross misrepresentation of the actual character of the climbing(?) in it. How far this misrepresentation is conscious it is not for us to say: it is possible that Messrs Kelsall and Hallitt are two of the most eminent and admirable climbers living. We merely record our deliberate opinion of this 'constant, interesting and sometimes difficult' (*sic*) climbing:—and it is based on our fairly intimate knowledge of the Cuillin up to and including Dearg: and take as standard, let us say, the most difficult bits in the accepted routes on Bidein, Mhadaidh, or Sgurr nan Gillean—none of which have ever yet given us occasion for the rope.

"We think that the pitches proper in this gully and certainly those up to the boss of the rock mentioned as dividing the gully are impossible from that standard; and we had to deal with conditions probably identical with that of Messrs Kelsall and Hallitt—'a certain quantity of water coming down the gully'. We spent in examining the pitches up to the boss of the rock 3–4 hours before we gave up the undertaking, and consider that the total absence of water would add little or nothing to the chances of climbing. We found several nailmarks on the rocks on the face adjoining the gully, and if the absence of nailmarks in the gully may be taken to indicate (as it is by the writers of the account) that no previous ascent had been made, *our* inability to find any such either justifies a similar inference over our gravest doubts."

To this Kelsall and Hallitt retorted:

"The politeness of the above is certainly beyond question but the whole of it is more a striking tribute to the abilities of the writers as carpers and sneering sceptics than as climbers."

Messrs Bell, Napier and Brown then entered the fray, and Bell wrote:

"We found the description of the gully by Messrs Kelsall and Hallitt most careful and accurate but owing to the unjustifiable and unsportsmanlike comments of Messrs Gray and Falcon we will give some details of our climb."

Which they did. But Falcon was not yet finished and added a later note:

"It appears that I have to thank Mr J. H. Bell for a new and original definition of the epithets 'justifiable' and 'unjustifiable', 'sportsmanlike' and 'unsportsmanlike'. So far from considering the mere independent statement of a definite and honest (however mistaken) opinion of any excursion narrated in this book as even mildly excusable, it is his pleasure to stigmatise such conduct by the second (in each case) of those coupled epithets. On the whole I consider this form of adjectival argument more fatal to the refuter than to the refuted. As regards the practical portion of his comment—that describing his own successful ascent, I shall be delighted (as doubtless will Mr Gray when he again appears on the scene, and can speak for himself) to take it as my guide in a second attempt in another (alas—the how manyeth?) note in this book—in case of repeated failure, for Mr Bell's delectation, in case of success, for his amazement."

While Gray had the final say:

"It was not my intention to begin a controversy. Two subsequent visits to the gully have merely confirmed my opinion as stated in that entry, which was written under the impression (left by their note) that Messrs Kelsall and Hallitt climbed the pitches proper. The larger of these I still consider impossible; and having now twice climbed Messrs Kelsall and Hallitt's route (with the exception of the last pitch) I am still of opinion that the climb, even by the sides and as compared with Moss Gyll, is singularly good and one requiring particular care. The rope may be used with advantage from the very bottom."

In rock climbing, however, we should be very diffident of using the word "impossible". No more than two years later that "impossible" pitch was climbed direct by members of the first Climbers' Club party to visit Skye. This consisted of R. E. Thomson, the brothers Slade and A. T. Fraser. After the usual opener of the Pinnacle Ridge they traversed the Basteir Tooth, were washed out of a camp in Harta Corrie, found the Inaccessible Pinnacle "eminently accessible", then turned their attention to the Waterpipe Gully.

They left Sligachan at 10 a.m., roped up at the foot of the gully at 1 p.m., reached the top at 1 a.m. and got back to Sligachan at 4.45 a.m., having been on the move for eighteen and a half hours.

Even yet very few parties do the climb without avoiding certain pitches and none would climb as high as Kelsall and Hallitt did without roping up. We are too apt to deride the standard of the pioneers—here certainly is a climb which has not become "an easy day for a lady".

The "impossible" eighty-foot pitch is really in two sections, a lower thirty-foot chimney crowned by a chokstone above which there is a stance and an

73

upper vertical chimney of forty feet or so. Under usual Skye conditions water cascades down the whole length of it.

When Abraham's party made the second direct ascent they reached the stance halfway up and contemplated the upper chimney:

"It looked frightfully steep and holdless and was adorned with the wettest waterfall under which we had ever shivered. About twenty feet up the chimney on the left wall was a rock ledge about a span of the fingers in width. From my shoulder Harland was able to attain this and wedged across the chimney to take in my rope till we were both seated side by side on the ledge with our feet on the opposite wall.

"The part above this ledge was very slimy and destitute of holds and Harland again used my shoulder to effect a higher lodgement. He was then entirely dependent on his own efforts for the rest of the pitch. With feet on the right wall and back on the other he worked his way slowly upward, testing every hold as some of them seemed loose, until a heavy rush of water announced the fact that he was out of its channel and safely at the top of the pitch."

Harland's suspicion that some of the holds were loose was borne out when the last man announced that the whole right wall of the chimney almost came down on him. On trying to dislodge loose stuff a huge mass of rock broke away and crashed down. Above this they encountered many other difficult pitches and of course were all soaked to the skin.

A. P. Abraham made his first visit to Skye in 1895 and was enthralled by the Cuillin. He was one of the not inconsiderable number who, with much experience of climbing in the Alps, infinitely preferred the peaks of Skye. His many visits resulted in a brilliant series of photographs, all taken on glass plates $8\frac{1}{2}$ inches by $6\frac{1}{2}$ inches in size and which are still available as postcards. Some are reproduced here and can hold their own with photographs of today in spite of all the advantages of modern technique and apparatus.

Abraham's party between the years 1895 and 1907 covered not only every peak, but every rock climb which had been done, whether in gully, on buttress, ridge or face, and pioneered many fine new routes. They made a second visit to the Waterpipe Gully to photograph the great pitch. When Harland and Binns were in position Abraham tied himself on to a pinnacle of rock overlooking the pitch, set up his camera in a very exposed position and proceeded to take the photograph. Scarcely had he done so when a gust of wind blew the camera over towards the gully. In clutching at it he lost his footing and swung into the void of the gully before the rope tightened round his waist. Fortunately he was able to regain his perch without injury to himself or his equipment (No. 49). Among new climbs by this party were the Spur and Summit Gullies of Sgurr an Fheadain and the Slanting Gully of Sgurr a' Mhadaidh.

The south face of the Inaccessible Pinnacle had been inviolate since W. W. King's exploration in 1895. He had the safeguard of a rope from above and his warning that the climb was unjustifiable without it deterred others. After Harland had led the Waterpipe Gully he thought himself fit for even an "unjustifiable" route and led it without much difficulty. Though very exposed throughout, the holds are thoroughly sound and hillwalkers who have gained the summit of Sgurr Dearg by the *easy route* will find it intensely thrilling to watch the ascent of this crack.

Abraham, who had also a good deal of experience of camping among the Cuillin in fair weather and in foul, also slept out in Coire Lagan without a tent. Of his many new routes two are particularly notable. The first of these was done while attempting to locate Dr Collie's route on the north face of Sgurr Alasdair and resulted in an entirely separate climb which keeps mostly to the edge overlooking the Great Stone Shoot, finishing right at the summit.

The other climb was that of the Cioch direct from Coire Lagan and which Abraham declared was the most memorable, the most exciting and just about the most difficult of any climb he had ever done over a long and strenuous rock-climbing career. Collie had conquered the Cioch by a flanking movement, first well away from it with a final descent from above. The reason for the avoidance of a frontal attack will be appreciated by anyone who looks up to the Cioch from below. There is a steep chimney for some distance, but this peters out with, above it, a mid-section of seemingly vertical rock. Appearances are often deceptive. Harland and Abraham roped up and Harland started up the chimney. By chimney, crack and face they wormed their way up, the climbing always difficult, and at one place Harland had to stand on Abraham's shoulders to gain a stance above. The only way onward was by way of two thin cracks about a yard apart which sprang upwards for ten feet or so. Harland proceeded cautiously, because, while the block between the two cracks was quite firm, he could not see what was holding it in place. As it was so big, weighing at least two tons, it was unlikely a man's weight would have any effect on it. After Harland found a belay in the chimney above the cracks

75

Abraham climbed up to him, treating the block between the cracks with great caution. This chimney had two small loose stones which Abraham thought better to dislodge. One of them hit the huge block below, which quivered, then broke away and thundered down, leaving in its wake a cloud of sulphurous dust.

Small wonder that Abraham recalls this as his most exciting climb, for they had just climbed over that very block, which had apparently been wedged in the cliffs for many, many years. Yet the slightest touch—for the loose stone only fell two feet—sent it downwards. There have been several other records of huge masses of rock coming away, but no one has had such a close shave as this.

Twenty-five years later J. E. B. Wright, a professional Lakeland Guide, described his ascent of the Cioch Direct:

"The concentration demanded by the next fifty feet drove everything from my mind except the certain knowledge that the difficulties I was grappling with required the utmost care in the management of my hands and feet. This was the nearest approach to the more severe granite type of climbing I had yet encountered in Skye.

"I was fifty feet above my companion, trying to find a way up an absolutely vertical groove. The four fingers of my left hand were in a deep, incut hold, my feet were resting on pressure-holds only, and both were awkwardly placed, and my right hand held a perpendicular hold in a crack known as a 'side-pull'. By raising both feet to higher pressure-holds and pulling sideways with my right hand my problem was to keep my balance and at the same time raise my body to full stretch until I could reach a very high hold with my left hand. I had already tried to perform this movement twice, only to find the high hold two inches beyond my reach. The strain of descending those few inches to my original position was very great and I was determined I should succeed at the third attempt. . . . Slowly and carefully I started on the hazardous movement. Everything was banished from my mind, except the desire to use all my strength and skill to reach that vital hold. The distance lessened till I was an inch away, now the tips of my fingers were level with it; slowly they closed over it and I grasped it in a frenzy of eagerness; now those four fingers took my weight whilst my feet came up and my right hand reached higher for another hold of adequate proportions; in the next

76

The Water-pipe Gully is much steeper than indicated in this photograph as seen in No. 49

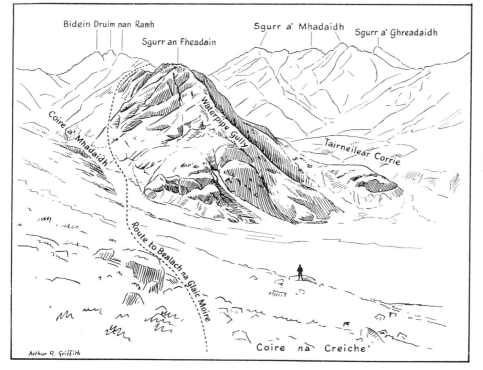

Bidein Druim nan Ramh

Sgurr an Fheadain

Sgurr a' Mhadaidh

Sgurr a' Ghreadaidh

Coire a' Mhadaidh

Waterpipe Gully

Tairneilear Corrie

Route to Bealach na Glaic Moire

Coire na Creiche

Arthur R. Griffith

39.
Coire na Creiche

40. Mary Campbell's cottage (Cuillin Cottage) was the first climbers' howff in Glen Brittle and countless climbers have enjoyed hospitality there since 1906

41. Mary herself taken about 1908. Mary died in 1947 and now her nephew and his wife carry on the good work

42. E. W. Steeple and A. H. Doughty inside Cuillin Cottage. In the early days the accommodation was rather primitive there being considerable congestion with climbers sleeping in a recess bed in the living-room. Now, of course, the cottage has been completely modernised, the recess bed is no more and this room is a comfortable lounge

43. Camp Coire Lagan, E. W. Steeple and Guy Barlow were the first climbers to explore the Cuillin from camps in the high corries. Steeple is the figure in each of the three photographs

44. Camp Coir' an Lochain

45. Camp Coir' a' Ghreadaidh

46.

47.

46. H. B. Buckle leading first attempt at Crack of Doom (1909)

47. E. W. Steeple and A. H. Doughty on East Buttress, Girdle Traverse of Sron na Ciche 1912

48. E. W. Steeple and Guy Barlow in Coire Lagan

49. Harland and Binns in the great 80-foot pitch of the Water-pipe Gully, 1907

50. Lochan Coir' a' Ghrundha, Sgurr Sgumain and Sgurr Alasdair

51. By the 1920's women climbers were common in Skye, and later all-women parties did all the great climbs
Evelyn Leach and Dalomie Cooper on the first pitch of White Slab route, Ghrundha Face of Sgurr Sgumain

52. Last pitch, White Slab route

moment I hauled myself into safety of a small recess and experienced that nervous and physical reaction which overtakes the mountaineer after moments of excessive strain."

This climb is now classified as severe and combined tactics are not employed.

A. P. Abraham had already published a book on rock climbing in North Wales and in 1908 appeared his *Rock Climbing in Skye*. The S.M.C. guide-book of the previous year was, of course, the first guide-book to the Cuillin, but it had only a small circulation and was already out of print. Abraham's book was much more complete and had the advantage of including a full description of Sron na Ciche, so soon to be known as the cragsman's playground. It reads cheerily today. The photographs illustrate the text very well, and, as will be seen, do not lose by comparison with those of today.

His book proved a great stimulus to climbing in Skye, leading to extensive exploration from its publication till 1914; so much so that scarcely any new routes were made elsewhere in Scotland. Year by year the climbers gathered at Sligachan. Everyone knew everyone else, for the mountaineering world was still a small world and some men were members of two, three and even four clubs. There was also a very definite social standing among the clubs, their members being almost entirely from the professional and wealthier classes.

Tourists were increasing. Still they were taken up and down Sgurr nan Gillean by obliging guides but seldom ventured elsewhere. Sgurr nan Gillean was the Matterhorn of Skye, the peak which "had to be climbed" and boasted about thereafter. What with tourists, artists and fishermen the climbers sometimes booked a year in advance at Sligachan to be sure of accommodation. Colin Phillip rented Glen Brittle Lodge every season, sometimes alone and sometimes with Collie. There he played genial host to climbers or arranged they should have the use of the lodge in his absence.

Others sought the cottage of the shepherd, Ewen Campbell, where his sister Mary reigned, and dispensed generous Highland hospitality. Countless climbers have happy memories of that little cottage nestling in trees by the burnside. Gaelic was Mary's mother-tongue. She thought in Gaelic, and when she came into the room, usually with another pot of tea, one could note she had been translating her comments into English on the way. (Nos. 40, 41, 42.)

Mary's cottage became very popular; many wrote of her great kindliness:

> *Though skies may weep or sun may shine*
> *In Skye the heavens vary;*
> *When home from mountain, glen or moor,*
> *There'll be a smile from Mary.*

"If in one short night one can have such wild admiration for Mary and her cottage, how very delightful the longer stays of the more fortunate must be."

Mary's teas were famous:

"Lingered in passing for a cup of tea. Then lingered on for four days of happiness and kindness from the kindliest of hostesses."

> *The masters of the hills at Slig*
> *Achan with all their climbing rig*
> *Are not so fortunate as ye,*
> *Whom Mary welcomes home to tea.*

> *Mary, fair maid of Glen Brittle,*
> *We thank you both not a little*
> *For comfort and care,*
> *The smile ever there*
> *And plenty of excellent victual.*

As to the weather climbers may take their choice:

"Sun shines eighteen hours a day."
"Consistently bad weather for ten days on end."
"Isle of Mist? I missed it—hot and sunny all the time."
"Weather perfect."
"Weather appalling."
"Three weeks perfect weather."
"Wonderful cloudless days."
"Bad weather, good time."

Climbers jumped at the chance of having a base so near the peaks. A goodly company of famous mountaineers have stayed at Mary's: E. W. Steeple, Guy Barlow, F. S. Goggs, P. J. H. Unna, H. MacRobert, W. Jeffrey, A. H. Doughty,

Harold Raeburn, Norman Collie, T. H. Somervell, Alex. Harrison, J. H. B. Bell, F. S. Smythe, A. W. Bridge are but a few of them.

In 1912 accommodation was made available at Glen Brittle post office, where Mrs Chisholm's hospitality equalled that of Mary Campbell. It is an enlightening commentary on the state of affairs that from 1912 right up till 1930 over seventy-five per cent of Mrs Chisholm's visitors were from south of the border.

These two cottages were quite small and often full up, so it is not surprising that campers increased in number. At one time or other tents have been pitched in almost every corrie of the Cuillin. One enterprising party hired a mule to transport their equipment to the chosen corrie. All went well till the animal came to its own croft, where it naturally decided to remain. Ultimately it was a case of the climber, instead of carrying his equipment up the hillside, hauling up the mule which carried it! At last the beast disposed of its burden and made off for home.

It is only when they have misadventures that we hear about the campers: when a rush of water forces evacuation or when the tent itself takes wings in a wild gust, leaving its lightly clad and shivering occupants on a waterproof sheet. Camping in Skye has no more drawbacks than camping elsewhere, and when the weather is set fair a camp in a high corrie is the most memorable part of a Cuillin holiday. There is a record of a party who camped for two weeks in the upper valley of Coruisk and, so perfect the weather, preferred to sleep out on the heather instead of in a tent.

It is an axiom that climbers who have once visited Skye must return "again and yet again". The S.M.C. stalwarts such as Rennie, Douglas, Ling, Maylard, Munro, Parker, Solly, Jeffrey and MacRobert were frequently to the fore, and it is worth recording the names of those who attended the largest pre-1914 war meet at Sligachan, twenty-five members in all: Backhouse, H. C. Boyd, Clapperton, W. I. Clark, Collins, Corry, Edwards, Garden, Glover, Goodeve, Howard, Howie, Levack, Ling, Maylard, Meares, Phillip, Reid, Rohde, Solly, Squance, Unna, H. Walker, White and Widdows.

Of the members of the English clubs none worshipped the Cuillin more devotedly than E. W. Steeple and Guy Barlow. While they also climbed in Wales and in Norway, Skye was their greatest love. With the exception of the war years they were in Skye almost every season from 1906 onwards. Occasionally they climbed with others, chiefly H. B. Buckle and A. H. Doughty, but most often together. No part of the Cuillin was unknown to them. They pioneered at least thirty "first ascents", including a great many new routes on Sron na Ciche and all the early routes in the Ghrunnda face of Sgurr Sgumain and Sgurr Alasdair.

H. B. Buckle was not a member of any climbing club, hence his doings have never been fully recorded. He was the first to appear on the scene, climbed in Skye from 1899 and introduced Barlow to the Cuillin in August 1906. Though there had been great climbing on Sron na Ciche by Collie's party during the previous month, they got no information from anyone in Glen Brittle. On August 8th Barlow and Buckle climbed to the Cioch by way of the Cioch gully and continued up the East Gully. Only on the climb did they notice the jutting-out crag, and were greatly surprised to find Collie's cairn on the top of it.

That evening they met Collie and intended to ask him what was known about Sron na Ciche, but he was so distant with them that neither said a word about their climb. It was not till the following year, when Barlow met Abraham in Wales, that he received from him information about Collie's first ascent and not till 1923 did he manage to obtain the exact date of Collie's climb. It is difficult to imagine such a thing happening in Glen Brittle today. Were a great new climb discovered the news would spread to everyone in the glen that very evening! Buckle and Barlow, therefore, ought to receive credit for an entirely independent discovery of the Cioch.

Another notable achievement was in 1909, when the same two explored the Crack of Doom, the most impressively named rock climb in Skye and well worth the title. After spending three and a half hours on the overhanging crack they were defeated just near the top and forced to retreat. Ten years went by before the first complete ascent was made by others. (No. 46.)

Steeple and Barlow introduced the words "girdle" into Skye climbing by making the historic girdle traverse of Sron na Ciche in 1912. This fine route goes from end to end of the precipice, maintaining an average level of about 2,250 feet and providing two thousand feet of first-class rock climbing. On a climb which is entirely an ascent a moderate second can climb behind an experienced leader, but on a traverse such as this both must be equally good. (No. 47.)

Over the years details of their adventures in Skye appeared from time to time in the *Climbers Club Journal*, the *Rucksack Club Journal* and the *Fell and Rock Club Journal*. Small wonder that the Scottish Mountaineering Club enticed them into its fold and gave them the job of editing their new guide-book to the Cuillin, together with MacRobert. This work they carried out with meticulous accuracy, Steeple being responsible for nearly all the new diagrams. It is characteristic of the men that, on their first visit to Skye after its publication, they promptly did a new route to make their own guide out of date!

Even Mary Campbell's cottage was not near enough to the climbs for them. With Doughty they camped out in Coir' a' Greadaidh, Coire Lagan and even lugged their tents to Coir' an Lochain and Coir' an Uaigneis, two of the most remote camping sites possible in the Cuillin. (Nos. 43, 44, 45.)

J. M. Archer Thomson and H. O. Jones, both legendary figures in the climbing world, put in an appearance in Skye in 1911. Archer Thomson, for the previous two decades, had been responsible for most of the new routes on Welsh hills and his guide-book to that area, which was published in 1910, was the first of modern rock-climbing guide-books. With Jones, a great scientist and leader in many a famous Alpine climb, he had just completed a most brilliant season in the Alps, so that both of them were at the peak of their form.

The other members of the party were Miss B. Jones, E. S. Reynolds, A. MacLaren and Leslie Shadbolt. Archer Thomson was then in his fiftieth year, yet could still lead severe rock climbs with grace and skill. Not for this party the known routes. In a week's brilliant *tour de force* they trod virgin rock every day, making six completely new ascents of a high standard of difficulty, and were impressed by the scale and quality of the climbing in the Cuillin— "excellent beyond all their experience in Britain".

MacLaren and Shadbolt were old campaigners in Skye, having climbed there since 1906. A great pair this: MacLaren the Celt who wore the kilt, played the bagpipes and had the Gaelic; and Shadbolt, famous among Welsh climbers and for his exploits on sea cliffs. He it was who suggested the possibility of a girdle traverse of the sea cliffs of the Isle of Sark, a supreme "girdle" surely, for it extends for twenty-five miles. On such cliffs he found limpets provided good holds for hands and feet. He had the idea of carrying limpets in his pockets and using them to provide holds where such were lacking on mainland hills. The limpets, however, refused to cling to alien rock.

Their first effort in Skye was a notable one. They saw the great black cleft which slants up the north face of the Basteir Tooth (photograph No. 38). Such is its forbidding appearance that no one ever thought of going near it. These two climbed it, and it proved more severe and with more complicated (and darker) inner passages than King's Cave Chimney beside it.

After such a start it is not surprising they conquered other new routes on Sron na Ciche and Sgurr nan Gillean. MacLaren was severely wounded at Loos in 1915 and did not climb after the war, but Shadbolt was back again with others to take part in the first ascent of the Crack of Doom, where Buckle and Guy Barlow had almost succeeded in 1909.

Not all of the famous visitors were intent on first ascents: the trodden routes and the glories of the ridges contented many. Geoffrey Winthrop Young obviously looked on the Cuillin to provide relaxation after his great campaigns in the Alps. Twice he stayed at Glen Brittle Lodge with Colin Phillip and climbed with Collie and Slingsby.

Conor O'Brien, the volatile Irishman who sailed round the world in a small boat, made a fleeting visit in 1912, and his name together with that of E. L. Julian appears on the roll of honour of first ascents. His approach was fitting, for he sailed his yacht from Dublin to Loch Scavaig, and must have been blessed with good weather when able to maintain an anchorage there.

Collie was over fifty by now; often he listened to discussions about new routes but did not venture information. After those concerned had departed he would say with a chuckle: "If they *do* get there they'll find a cairn."

Came the war in 1914 calling climbers to stern tasks. Many never returned. Many were never again to see the Hebridean sunset; to feel the fingers tingle to the rasp of the gabbro.

Access to Skye was difficult during the war years; comparatively few visitors reached the island. N. E. Odell was wounded at the Battle of Vimy in 1917 and got married when sent home on sick leave. Where a remoter spot from the horrors of war than the Isle of Skye? There he went for final convalescence and honeymoon. For several weeks of wild autumn weather he and his wife roamed the Skye hills together, and even as early as October found snow and ice on the Inaccessible Pinnacle, up which Odell cut steps with a geological hammer. Odell admits that he learned much on the incomparable gabbro of the Cuillin, and of the Everest band of climbers he and Howard Somervell had been the most faithful to the hills of Skye.

George Mallory came, that very Galahad of the mountains who was destined to become one of the immortals. With early training on Welsh hills, introduced, when still a boy, to the Alps by R. L. G. Irving, he had behind him a splendid record of achievement and leadership. Denied the Alps for four years, he sought the peaks of the Cuillin, there to gird on again his armour of mountaincraft. There he started off on the final stage which was to lead him again to the Alps, then to the Himalaya and finally higher than man had ever gone before, perhaps to the summit of Mount Everest.

Mallory, with his wife, Leslie Shadbolt and D. R. Pye, had a fortnight in Skye in the summer of 1918. For them the weather gods stage-managed things perfectly. For the first two days they climbed through swirling mists which momently would clear to reveal dark corrie or black peak. Only when they reached the summits did the mist lift to reward them with a panorama of the whole mighty range.

although there are only three difficult movements, the climb is very steep & there are not many belays. It may be noted that the first ascent was made under perfect conditions.

July. 28ᵗ 1918

D. R. Pye.
G. H. L. Mallory
Ruth Mallory.
L. G. Shadbolt.

MALLORY'S ENTRY IN SLIGACHAN CLIMBERS' BOOK

Then followed ten days of perfect weather, each day hotter than the last. After a new climb on Sgurr a' Mhadaidh the party moved over to Glen Brittle to enjoy abundant hospitality at Mrs Chisholm's. Sron na Ciche became their playground. They seem to have covered most of the standard routes. Some are against giving climbs personal names, but we should be proud that the name of such a man as Mallory is permanently enshrined on Sron na Ciche. He it was who first led with great care and skill the Slab and Groove route, which is now much more often called Mallory's route.

The war over, climbers sought the Cuillin once more. 1919 brought Dorothy Pilley, then serving her novitiate, and later to be known as one of the finest of women climbers, together with C. F. Holland and H. E. C. Carr. The party approached Glen Brittle from Loch Slapin and discovered, as many others have discovered to their dismay, that Camasunary, which looms so large on the map, is *not* the expected village and that no supplies are obtainable. On the map the journey from Loch Slapin to Glen Brittle seems quite simple. Many have been lured that way. One lot thought so little of it that they carried no food, to arrive at Glen Brittle in an exhausted condition after a journey lasting three days. Of course it can be done in one day, but not, as with Miss Pilley's party, if much time is spent climbing Blaven and bathing at Camasunary.

They were overtaken by darkness and spent the night by the shores of Loch Scavaig. Many fine climbs were made subsequently, of which the best was the Cioch west route.

In 1920 Harland was back again, this time with George Abraham, and led a new route on Knight's Peak of Sgurr nan Gillean; while the following year A. S. Piggott and J. Wilding discovered still other two ways to ascend the Inaccessible Pinnacle.

Still the most constant visitors were Steeple and Barlow. From 1919 they seemed to be almost permanent summer residents at Mary Campbell's cottage. When a series of large parcels, just within the postal limits, started to arrive, Glen Brittle knew Steeple and Barlow would follow. Gear, provisions, equipment, all came by this means, to the considerable embarrassment of the local postman. But that was a mere trickle compared with the deluge of twenty years later, when hundreds sought Glen Brittle and when every item of food, including bread, had to be sent in advance, so that Mrs Chisholm's little post office was often stacked to the roof with parcels of every size and description.

So many new climbs fell to this pair that, if they were seen near a promising crag, it was fairly safe to assume it would soon be scratched by hobnailed boots. The Chasm of Sgurr nan Eag was one of their more spectacular captures, but their main efforts were on the Ghrunnda faces of Sgurr Sgumain and Sgurr Alasdair.

In 1923 the publication of the S.M.C. Guide to Skye proved their unique knowledge of the Cuillin. It gave details of so many routes which had never previously been noted that it had the effect of stifling the search for further new ways. Climbers wanted to follow in the steps of the experts and experience for themselves the thrills of the routes so graphically described by text, photographs and diagrams. Sron na Ciche was now criss-crossed with routes and it was thought that rock climbing in Skye had reached its peak, with but little chance for further exploration. (No. 33.)

The years which followed the publication of the Guide seemed to prove this. Only about six first-class routes were made between then and 1939.

How are new climbs discovered? The most usual method nowadays is for climbers to examine rock-climbing guide-books and to note areas of crags with no marked route. This was the method used by Alan Horne and H. V. Hughes. A close study of the 1923 diagram of Sron na Ciche indicated a blank area. They promptly went to explore it, and their exploration resulted in a fine new climb known as the Amphitheatre Wall.

The second method was that of J. H. B. Bell and F. S. Smythe. One evening in 1924, from Glen Brittle post office, they noticed a long vertical shadow on the face of Sgurr Sgumain which indicated some sort of fault and where there was no known route. Exploration yielded the Trap Face Climb, which is unique in that it has a stairway of basalt. Collie had discovered the Cioch by similar revealing evening shadows twenty years previously.

A third method is that of D. L. Reid's party. They had no intention of making a new route and started up what they took to be the well-known West Central Gully. Only when they were a considerable way up did they discover they were on an entirely new route, now known as the Engineer's Slant.

Frankland's Gully of Sgurr Sgumain was a somewhat similar sort of mistake. The party intended to do one of the face climbs on Sgurr Alasdair. Mist led them astray, and when they proceeded to climb it they arrived on the summit of Sgurr Sgumain instead of Sgurr Alasdair. These are the usual methods, but in the Cuillin there was, round about the 'twenties, still another way. Collie's companions, particularly Colin Philip and John Mackenzie, in their enthusiasm, at times attributed to Collie climbs which he had not done. Thus Phillip told Barlow of a grand climb on the Eastern Buttress of Sron na Ciche which, he said, Collie had pioneered. Years later Steeple and Barlow climbed it and found that theirs *was* the first ascent! Other new routes were also made on Sgurr Sgumain and Sron na Ciche and one on Sgurr na h-Uamha.

Up till about 1930 the pattern of Skye climbing continued as previously. Members of English clubs continued to come in increasing numbers, while a new club, the Midland Association of Mountaineers, based on Birmingham, was founded in 1922. As Steeple and Barlow were concerned in its foundation its members soon got to know the Cuillin. The S.M.C., as formerly, held Easter or summer meets at Sligachan every few years, and the ranks of Scottish climbers were reinforced by the Junior Mountaineering Club of Scotland (1926). Yet still the climbers were of the same social status. A great change was on the way.

THE GREAT TRAVERSE

The main ridge of the Cuillin extends for eight miles from north to south, comprising eighteen peaks, some of which have several tops. All are linked together and nowhere does the ridge descend below two thousand five hundred feet. (No. 16.)

No sooner had climbers got to know every part of it than they started to wonder if the whole ridge could be done in one day. At first the suggestion aroused incredulity, for had not Collie taken eighteen hours to explore the section between Sgurr a' Mhadaidh and Sgurr Thearlaich? William Brown in 1896 considered it a feat only for the gods, who could step from mountain top to mountain top, and thought ordinary mortals would require three long summer days.

As greater acquaintance was made with the range this subject was the more often discussed, but no one attempted to prove the point. Then, in 1904, the climbing world was astounded by the fell-walking feat of A. W. Wakefield. Starting and returning to Keswick he ascended Scafell Pike, Helvellyn, Skiddaw and many of the other intervening peaks, including Bow Fell, Great End, Fairfield and Saddleback, in nineteen hours fifty-three minutes. The following year he added still more summits, covering 23,500 feet of ascent and descent in twenty-two hours seven minutes. This record stood till 1920, when it was broken by Eustace Thomas and later by Robert Graham of Keswick.

These were tremendous feats of endurance but after all they were *walks*, while there are few parts of the Cuillin ridge which can be described as easy walking; in many parts both hands and feet are constantly employed, with four sections of rock climbing far above the easy standard. In Lakeland the fell walker could always quench his thirst (about ten miles to a pint, as one wag has it); on the Cuillin main ridge water would have to be carried. On Lakeland hills the compass would put one right should mist come down. On the Cuillin magnetic rocks make the compass unreliable and there are accessory ridges to lure the wanderer from the straight and narrow path.

Some considered it utterly impossible, while others thought it might be done some day but only by super-climbers. Abraham agreed with the latter group but doubted if any climber would ever have the various qualifications necessary to ensure success:

"He would need to have exceptional physique and staying power, to be a quick, skilful, and neat rock climber (particularly would he require to be neat, otherwise his hands would be torn to pieces before he got halfway); to possess an intimate knowledge of the entire range and familiarity with the various difficult sections, while perfect weather, a light rope to 'double' for descents and a carefully arranged commissariat would be necessary."

86

The appearance of the above in Abraham's book caused even more discussion and several parties made tentative plans. Geoffrey Winthrop Young and A. M. Mackay might well have had the honour. Their records both at home and in the Alps leave no doubt that they could have managed it had not Mackay had the misfortune to break a leg in Arran before the planned assault.

By winter fireside others were dreaming of it, working out approximate times and difficulties, arguing as to the amount of food to be carried. The climbers examine the problem thus—from Glen Brittle three miles of very, very rough walking, followed by an ascent of 2,934 feet by seemingly interminable scree slopes to the summit of Gars-bheinn, the most southern peak. Rough scrambling over Sgurr a' Choire Bhig, followed by a dip and an ascent of five hundred feet to reach the first Munro, Sgurr nan Eag, 3,037 feet. A little rough going over Caisteal a' Garbh-choire and on to Sgurr Dubh na Da Bheinn. Care required here in mist, lest one follow the accessory ridge eastwards to Loch Coruisk. Easy descent to Bealach Coir' an Lochain, beyond which is the first real difficulty, the Thearlaich-Dubh gap. Rope up for rock climbing, down the short side and up the long side of the gap, then on to summit of Sgurr Thearlaich, then descent by steep slabs to the col between it and Sgurr Mhic Coinnich. Difficult rock climbing by King's Chimney to summit of latter, easy descent to Bealach Coire Lagan, then hard plug of five hundred feet to the Inaccessible, which has to be traversed up the long side and down the short side. Probably take off the rope now. Rough scrambling now four tops of Sgurr na Banachdich, Sgurr Thormaid, the two tops of Sgurr a' Ghreadaidh and the four tops of Sgurr a' Mhadaidh, with still rougher going over three peaks of Bidein Druim nan Ramh. Easy going to Bruach na Frithe and on till the Basteir Tooth blocks the way. Rock climbing again—and another awkward pitch to summit of Am Basteir. The end in sight now, for there is the narrow west ridge of Sgurr nan Gillean with the "policeman" blocking the way. From Sgurr nan Gillean the "easy" route of three miles to Sligachan. Taken altogether seven miles on the ridges with ten thousand feet of ascent and eight miles to and from the ridges.

Thus did many parties work it out, till at last one pair were brave enough to test themselves. Leslie Shadbolt and A. C. MacLaren first climbed in Skye in 1906. Though they made other visits after that there were still large sections unknown to them in 1911. Hence they did not fulfil one of Abraham's qualifications, though certainly they were bold and resolute climbers. Nor did they bother to lay caches of food at strategic parts of the ridge as many deemed necessary. That they were fast travellers is shown by the fact that they reached the summit of Gars-bheinn in two and a half hours from Glen Brittle. As they had allowed themselves four hours for this section they had beaten bogey and were much cheered. MacLaren set the pace and timed everything meticulously, even noting that they took *one* minute to rope up before crossing the Thearlaich-Dubh gap. Sgurr Alasdair, the highest point, is not actually on the main ridge, but of course it had to be included, which meant a slight diversion. The round of Coire Lagan delayed them owing to their unfamiliarity with Sgurr Thearlaich and Sgurr Mhic Coinnich. After traversing the Inaccessible

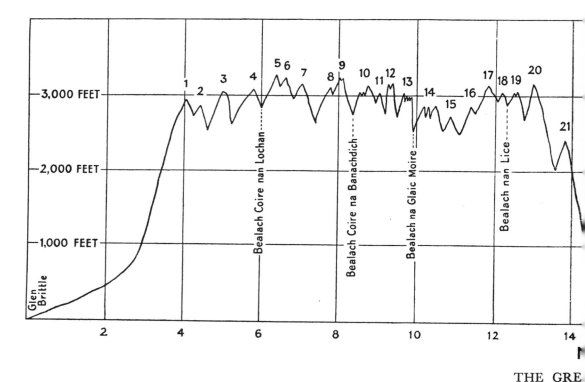

THE GRE

1. Gars-bheinn.
2. Sgurr a' Choire Bhig.
3. Sgurr nan Eag.
4. Sgurr Dubh na Da Bheinn.
5. Sgurr Alasdair.
6. Sgurr Thearlaich.

7. Sgurr Mhic Coinnich.
8. An Stac.
9. Sgurr Dearg and Inaccessible.
10. Sgurr nan Banachdich.
11. Sgurr Thormaid.
12. Sgurr a' Ghreadaidh.

on the rope they found themselves at the summit of Sgurr Dearg two and a half hours ahead of their schedule. This boosted their morale still further and they rested and smoked for three-quarters of an hour.

After that they traversed the next five peaks within two hours. Thirst was bothering them now and they were anxious to reach the pool of water near the ridge at Sgurr a' Fhionn Choire. That spot was not reached till 5 p.m. and the ascent of the Basteir Tooth by Naismith's route seemed hard at the end of fourteen hours. That over they travelled well on over Sgurr nan Gillean and reached Sligachan, sixteen hours forty-five minutes after they had left Glen

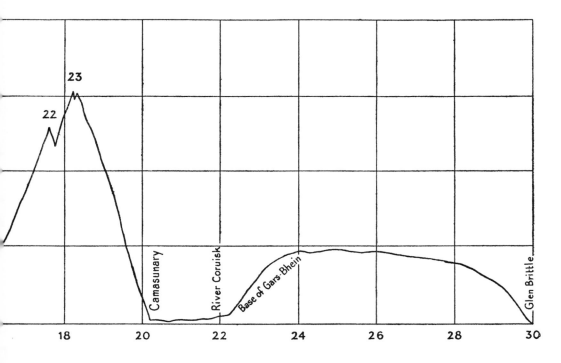

VERSE

13. Sgurr a' Mhadaidh.
14. Bidein Druim nan Ramh.
15. An Caisteal.
16. Sgurr na Bhairnich.
17. Bruach na Frithe.
18. Sgurr a' Fhionn Choire.
19. Am Basteir and Basteir Tooth.
20. Sgurr nan Gillean.
21. Sgurr na h-Uamha.
22. Clach Glas.
23. Blaven.

Brittle, halts at various points of the ridge having occupied two and a half hours of this time.

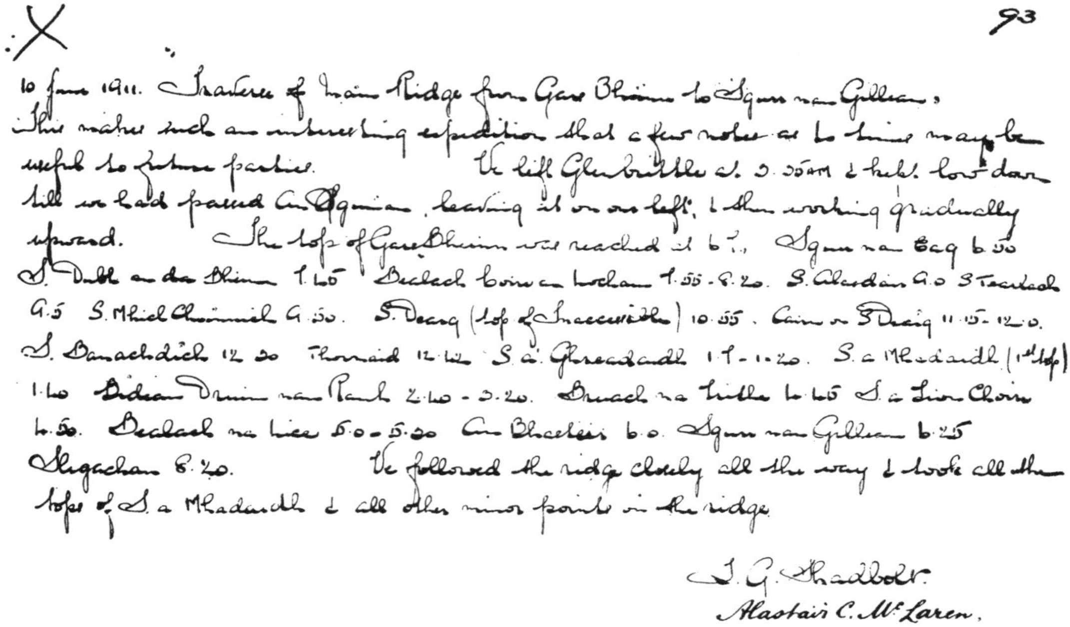

✗   93

[Handwritten entry, facsimile:]

10 June 1911. Traverse of main Ridge from Gars Bheinn to Sgurr nan Gillean. This makes such an interesting expedition that a few notes as to times may be useful to future parties. We left Glenbrittle at 5.55 a.m. & held low down till we had passed An Sguman, leaving it on our left, & then working gradually upward. The top of Gars Bheinn was reached at 6.7., Sgurr na Beag 6.30 S. Dubh an da Bheinn 7.40 Bealach Coire an Lochain 7.55-8.20. S. Alasdair 9.0 Sgurr Thearlaich 9.5 S. Mhic Choinnich 9.50. S. Dearg (top of Inaccessible) 10.55. Cairn na S Dearg 11.15-12.0. S. Banachdich 12.20 Thormaid 12.40 S. a Ghreadaidh 1.9-1.20. S. a Mhadaidh (1st top) 1.40 Bidean Druim nan Ramh 2.40-3.20. Bruach na Frithe 4.45 S. a Fionn Choire 4.55. Bealach na Lice 5.0-5.20 Am Bhasteir 6.0 Sgurr nan Gillean 6.25 Sligachan 8.40. We followed the ridge closely all the way & took all the tops of S. a Mhadaidh & all other minor points in the ridge

J. G. Shadbolt.
Alastair C. M.Laren.

SHADBOLT AND MACLAREN'S ENTRY IN SLIGACHAN CLIMBERS' BOOK

This party certainly found the traverse well within their powers and it seemed it would be within the capabilities of many other climbers. Yet, though unstinted praise was given to the two heroes, no others followed in their footsteps up till 1920.

In June 1920 T. H. Somervell and his brother had a climbing holiday in Scotland, rightly reserving the Cuillin as the final tit-bit. The Waterpipe Gully, the Cioch Direct, and the Crack of Doom they took in their stride, and T. H., feeling in perfect condition, sought a companion for the traverse when his brother had to go home. Graham Wilson of a Fell and Rock party, agreed and they started from Glen Brittle at 7 a.m. one morning. Gars-bheinn was reached within two hours, half an hour better than the original party. Graham Wilson gave up the struggle on Sgurr na Banachdich and descended to Glen Brittle. Somervell strode on, making the mountains shrink beneath his feet, though he suffered much from thirst on such a hot and windless day. So fresh did he feel on Sgurr nan Gillean that he included Sgurr na h-Uamha in the excursion and reached Sligachan in fourteen and a quarter hours. He thought it the finest expedition outside the Alps and declared that, with a water-bottle and a pound of raisins, he could better the time by an hour.

Most climbers would have rested the next day. Not so Somervell who secured another companion and climbed the Slanting Gully of Sgurr a' Mhadaidh and part of the ridge on the way back to Glen Brittle. That Somervell's performance was an excellent one was proved by his splendid achievements on Mount Everest a few years later.

Both these traverses were from south to north, so it was inevitable that some one should try it from north to south. This duly happened in July 1924, the climbers being B. R. Goodfellow and F. Yates of the Rucksack Club. Probably it is rather harder when done in this direction, as the three sections where rock climbing is necessary come towards the end of the day, while the short side of the Thearlaich-Dubh gap is more difficult to ascend than descend. Their time was seventeen hours, a very fine show indeed, as they were in thick mist all the time and hence had the added worry of route-finding.

While these two were on the ridge F. S. Smythe and J. H. B. Bell were in Glen Brittle planning the attempt. Smythe was then acquiring the reputation which was ultimately to make him one of the finest mountaineers of his time, while Bell, now over fifty, is still finding and leading new routes of great severity.

BELL'S AND SMYTHE'S ENTRY IN SLIGACHAN CLIMBERS' BOOK.

Profiting from Somervell's remarks about thirst, they took with them a length of rubber tubing by which the least rock pool could be sucked dry, while Smythe did the whole traverse wearing crepe rubber shoes, which were almost worn out by the time they reached Sgurr nan Gillean. Their time was much the same as that of Shadbolt and MacLaren.

By this time women were taking an increasing share in Cuillin-climbing, though the Islefolk were slow to appreciate them. As recently as 1921 the manageress of Sligachan Inn shook with fear at the very idea of Dorothy Pilley entering the dining-room wearing climbing breeches. (Nos. 51, 52.)

The Pinnacle Club—an all-women club—was formed in 1921 and soon its members were disporting themselves in Skye. Though a party were washed out and benighted on their first excursion in 1924, Skye had them in its thrall. In 1925 a larger mixed party returned and camped in a rude hut then in existence by Loch Scavaig near Loch Coruisk.

Inevitably the main ridge traverse was discussed and the strategic position of the hut pointed out. The Cuillin main ridge being in the form of a horseshoe and Glen Brittle being near one end on the *outer* side means that you are travelling *further* from Glen Brittle all the time. On the other hand, the Scavaig hut being on the *inner* side of the horseshoe, by keeping to the ridge you would be *returning* to it. Thus the double prospect—the party to include the first female, and to return to the starting-point the same day, a thing no previous climbers had done.

A party of six left a camp in Coir' a' Ghreadaidh, climbed to the ridge at the Inaccessible, where they left a cache of food, before descending to the hut at Loch Scavaig. The chosen lady, Miss M. M. Barker, and her accomplices, H. V. Hughes and C. D. Frankland, started off at 5.30 a.m. the next morning to encounter thick mist and a very strong wind on the ridge. Instead of a climbing rope they carried a clothes line for lowering rucksacks, though it appears that, owing to abnormal conditions, it was used for other purposes. On the Inaccessible Pinnacle rain came pelting down; nothing now but a retreat to Loch Scavaig. That was easier said than done, for Bealach Coire na Banachdich, the only pass which they knew, had disappeared! Seven times they started off from the summit of Sgurr Dearg and seven times returned to it after various wanderings in thick mist with the compass behaving like a mad thing. Ultimately they gave up the struggle, retraced their steps over Sgurr Dearg to Bealach Coire Lagan and descended from there, reaching camp after seventeen hours.

Back they came in August 1926, made a cache on the ridge and provisioned the Scavaig hut for five days. The climbing party was now reduced to Miss Barker and C. D. Frankland, with Gertrude Walmsley and Edith Davies in support. Two days of bad weather made them desperate. The third day was the last chance before the end of their holiday. Off they went for Gars-bheinn at 5 a.m. Mist till Sgurr Dearg, then it lifted suddenly, and thereafter the Cuillin regaled them with brands of weather varying from brilliant sunshine to storms of hail and rainbows. At 8.30 p.m. they were on Sgurr nan Gillean and had a race to get off Sgurr na h-Uamha before darkness. Light was gone six miles from camp, but they were on easy ground by that time and reached the hut at 1 a.m.—twenty hours out. This was a longer excursion than any previous one, involving at least eighteen miles plus ten thousand feet of ascent. They kept strictly to the crest of the ridge all the time and did not carry a rope, which reveals a very high standard of climbing and endurance on the part of the female member of the party.

Still the Pinnacle Club hankered for a traverse planned and carried out entirely by themselves. Another party—all women this time—reached Skye at Whitsun 1927 and installed themselves with Mrs MacRae. The first few days were spent traversing those parts of the ridge with which they were unacquainted and making two caches, one of food at the foot of the Inaccessible and another of food and spare woollies at Bealach na Glaic Moire. With a party of four they calculated they might well require the round of the clock, hence the woollies in case they had to spend the hours of darkness on the ridge.

On the chosen day they got up at 5 a.m. Heavy rain—back to bed! Next day brought better weather and they were off at 9 a.m. after a very satisfying breakfast. The party consisted of Lilian Bray, Dr Corbett and T. and B. Wells, and they took the usual route over the moor to Gars-bheinn and northwards along the ridge. As happens so often in the Cuillin, the weather belied its early promise, a snow and hail storm battering them on the Thearlaich-Dubh gap. After that it continued cold with frequent still colder showers. Instead of King's Chimney on Sgurr Mhic Coinnich they took the easier route by Collie's Ledge and ascended and descended the Inaccessible by the longer east ridge. By that time it was 9 p.m. and bitterly cold. They kept on for two more hours until weariness and darkness called a halt. This was on Sgurr a' Ghreadaidh, with their spare woollies, so much needed, still several peaks ahead. Hours of darkness were spent on the rain- and wind-swept ridge, huddled together in pairs, the cold being such that water was frozen in their water-bottle in the morning. By 3 a.m. they were on the move again, still feeling cold, while the rocks were glazed with ice and thick mist all around. Half an hour was enough. The decision to give up the struggle was unanimous; they left the ridge at Sgurr a' Mhadhaidh and got back to Glen Brittle by 6 a.m.

Such an experience would have daunted most folk. Not so the Pinnacle stalwarts—it only made them the more eager to complete the job. On the next Whitsun (1928) they returned to the attack, the party being the same except for Dr Corbett. Caches of food were laid as previously and they got away by 2.30 a.m. With only three in the party progress was faster and they reached the Inaccessible nine and a half hours out. Intense cold had defeated them the previous year; now intense heat was the enemy, with the rocks almost too hot to touch. Though they had a good supply of oranges, throats became parched up; they were barely able to speak. All afternoon the sun beat down remorselessly, for there is no shade on the Cuillin ridge. Progress became slower and slower. At 9 p.m. they were toiling up towards Bruach na Frithe when one of them announced she could go no further. All three lay down in their tracks and this time they managed to sleep a little. On the move at 2.30 a.m., they reached Sgurr nan Gillean at 9 a.m., having been thirty and a half hours without water, got to Sligachan at 11 a.m. and walked back over the bealach to Glen Brittle in the afternoon.

Women having done the traverse, men lost interest and four years went by before there was another attempt. Then in August 1932, Peter Bicknell astonished the climbing world by bringing the time down to eleven hours fifty-seven minutes. Of this time eight hours was spent on the actual ridge, compared with Somervell's ten and a half hours.

Interest was aroused again. Many parties have done it since then and still more parties have failed in the attempt.

In June 1935 J. H. B. Bell became the first man to do the traverse twice. On this occasion he was accompanied by C. M. Allan and they included Sgurr Dubh Mor and Sgurr Sgumain, two peaks on secondary ridges and which were not climbed by any of the other parties. They also returned direct to Glen Brittle from Sgurr nan Gillean without descending to Sligachan.

Not to be outdone, Peter Bicknell also made a second traverse, this time with his brother and with no thought of a new record.

Some parties had bad luck, such as G. R. Symmons and W. A. Emery, who had to give up at Bealach nan Lice with only one more peak to bag, and G. F. Peaker and C. D. Milner, who encountered a terrific storm when approaching the Basteir Tooth and had to omit it. These parties came very near to success, while most of the others who failed gave up the struggle halfway. It does indeed require considerable strength of will to continue when one is seven or eight hours out, when a scorching sun beats down and one is parched by thirst, and when from Sgurr Dearg or Sgurr na Banachdich one can see clear cool pools in the corrie below. Or should it be storm or mist the magnet of the comfort of Mary Campbell's, Mrs Chisholm's or Glen Brittle Lodge is difficult to resist when they can be reached within an hour.

As years went by more and more parties made the traverse and now scarce a mountaineering club in Britain but can claim among its members those who have done so. Latterly the ridge became so common that climbers did not bother to note their times on each peak, merely stating total time Glen Brittle to Sligachan or vice versa, times varying from fourteen to twenty hours. W. H. Murray first did the traverse in 1937 and has now done it three times, while W. L. Wood, with the advantage of living in Skye, has done it five times. Cyril Machin claims that the best way is to start after breakfast on a June morning, take it leisurely with plenty of rests, aiming to arrive at Sligachan about breakfast-time the following morning. I prefer his second traverse when the climbers were met at two places on the ridge by supporting parties carrying hot drinks and food, thus making the traverse something of a de luxe expedition.

University mountaineers have been very active in Skye of recent years and their members have been responsible for many traverses, the most notable that by G. C. Band of Cambridge, who did the traverse in fifteen and a half hours, starting and finishing at Camasunary. Both he and Sydney Thomson have cut down even Peter Bicknell's remarkable ridge time. At the time of going to press Dan Stewart of Edinburgh appears to hold the record for the ridge time from Gars-bheinn to Sgurr nan Gillean, completing it in 1950 in six hours forty-five minutes.

At least eight climbers did it in 1951 and two more ladies have their names on this roll of fame.

This climb has gone the way of all climbs. At first it was thought utterly impossible, then it was conceded it could be done by supermen among climbers, till at last Dorothy Hudson, a young girl of seventeen with but three months climbing experience, accomplished it without much difficulty and – the crowning insult – she did it wearing hiking shorts.

95

The Cuillin of Skye

THE GREATER TRAVERSE

Always the ridge walkers had tantalising glimpses of Blaven and Clach Glas across Glen Sligachan. They stood as a challenge and brought a sense of incompleteness. Wouldn't it be a magnificent finish up to the expedition to include these other two peaks and all within twenty-four hours? Could it be done? On the main ridge climbers do not descend below two thousand five hundred feet, but to reach Blaven they would have to descend almost to sea-level, walk through Glen Sligachan and face an extra four thousand feet of ascent at the end of a long, hard day. In 1920 Somervell thought it possible but did not make the attempt. Yet he planted the germ of the idea which took twenty years to mature.

In 1938 I met Ian Charleson of Edinburgh at Zermatt and we had many happy days of climbing together. During a halt on the Riffelhorn, where we were putting in some training for the Matterhorn traverse, the talk turned to the Cuillin—as always it will do, even in the great Alps. Ian pointed out that the ridge plus Blaven and Clach Glas had never been done and that Bell, during a recent lecture, had said it was high time someone was doing something about it. Though he did not say so openly, I gathered he was thinking about it himself, and I saw enough of him during that holiday to appreciate that such an expedition was within his powers.

I was not too surprised, therefore, when I received a postcard from Sligachan the following June announcing his triumph and thus ensuring both himself and his companion, W. E. Forde, a place among the immortals of the climbing world. Only later did I learn all details. Probably no ridge expedition was planned so carefully as this one. Everything had been carefully worked out the previous winter, though, fearing they would be forestalled or thought ambitious fools, they kept their plans to themselves.

Their final plan involved the use of three tents, one for the main camp, one which they would pitch at the foot of Gars-bheinn and a third in Harta Corrie. This third camp they considered the linch-pin of the whole scheme. Its purpose was twofold—to enable them to have a rest and a meal under cover after descending from Sgurr na h-Uamha and before setting off on the final lap to Blaven, while it would also welcome them on their return and so save them many weary miles of bog marching to Sligachan.

Their first week was spent traversing various parts of the ridge, laying caches of food at the Inaccessible and pitching and provisioning the two extra tents.

96

At 1.30 a.m. on June 11th they left their camp and started up Gars-bheinn. Though almost midsummer there was plenty of evidence of overnight frost. Tufts of moss were frozen and some of the rocks had a thin coating of ice, which is all added proof of the oft-repeated statement that it may be winter any day of the year on Scottish hills. Winter clothing was worn—wind-proof breeches and anoraks, Balaclava helmets and woollen gloves. On the ridge it was very cold and windy and from Sgurr Alasdair to Sgurr a' Ghreadaidh it shamelessly snowed. All continued well and the dull wintry weather was probably a help rather than a hindrance, thirst not being such an enemy. These two fed better than any previous ridge walkers, having two good meals on the way. Even so they felt mighty tired when descending to their tent in Harta Corrie and were doubtful if they could go further. A rest for an hour and a half and another good feed worked wonders, so that they started off up Glen Sligachan in the evening, reached the summit of Clach Glas as darkness was beginning to fall and Blaven at 11.5 p.m.—just over twenty hours from the summit of Gars-bheinn.

In one way the record made by Charleson and Forde will never be beaten, for they carried with them a full-size alarm clock and set it whenever they sat down to rest in case they fell asleep. To beat that record a party would have to do the Greater Traverse carrying with them a grandfather clock.

The unattainable had been attained, the trail had been blazed. Others were quick to follow.

A month later J. K. Cooke, F. B. Dutton Walker and C. McGavin of the Wayfarers' Club left camp in Glen Sligachan at 8 p.m., and because of darkness found the route to Blaven rather tricky, but got there by 11.40 p.m.

They descended to Camasunary, missed the stepping stones-across the river, had to wade through three feet of water and constantly lost the track the whole way round to Loch Scavaig. About 6 a.m. they reached the summit of Gars-bheinn, where they had cached food previously. On the ridge walk north they took in Sgurr Dubh Mor and Sgurr Sgumain, broached their second cache on Sgurr Dearg at 2 p.m. and finally reached Sgurr nan Gillean at 9 p.m. They were therefore the first party to climb all the Skye *Munros* in one day.

Of course such feats were bound to attract Bill Murray, then just beginning to acquire his reputation as a cragsman and a leader. He and R. G. Donaldson managed to get off to Skye that August. Starting from Glen Brittle at 9.30 p.m., they traversed the ridge in mist and darkness by torchlight as far as the

97

Thearlaich-Dubh gap. Thereafter they had sunshine. No caches had been made; they subsisted on bread sandwiches for the first ten hours and carried one and a half pints of water. At their previously provisioned tent in Glen Sligachan they fed and rested and then traversed Clach Glas and Blaven in good style, cutting down the top-to-top time by one hour.

This party's diet was a novel departure from precedent. At the tent in the glen they each drank half a pint of "Mummery's blood", a now classical climbers' drink consisting of equal parts Navy rum and Bovril served hot, which according to Murray is "nourishing, warming, strengthening and lowers angles, shortens distances and improves weather". After their sandwiches were finished they consumed at intervals tablets of vita-glucose, which they praised highly, noting a definite improvement in muscular efficiency.

A variation of the greater expedition was by B. H. Simmonds, R. Tomsett and L. Chapman, who slept out on the summit of Blaven and then did the main ridge from north to south. Instead of going on to Gars-bheinn they bagged Sgurr Dubh Mor and Sgurr Sgumain, thus being the second party to cover all the Cuillin peaks over three thousand feet in one day.

But, said the critics, to complete the job you ought to return to your starting point within twenty-four hours. This was thought utterly impossible, as the best top-to-top time was nineteen hours, while the journey from Glen Brittle to Gars-bheinn would take two hours and the long trek from Blaven back to Glen Brittle about six hours.

In June 1944 J. M. Edwards did the impossible by completing the expedition Glen Brittle to Glen Brittle in twenty-four hours exactly. Here was a man who in the years before the war had pioneered a great number of very severe rock climbs in Snowdonia, who was recognised as one of our greatest leaders and whose guide-book to Cwm Idwal is a classic. Only such a man could afford to treat the Cuillin so casually. He had not been over much of the ridge previously, while caches of food or tents did not occur to him. He did not even carry a watch, hence knew only starting and finishing times. No glucose for Edwards! He just took the usual packet of sandwiches supplied to climbers at Glen Brittle House, started off at 8.30 a.m. one morning and followed the ridge from Gars-bheinn to Sgurr nan Gillean. Only then did he decide to bag Blaven also, not knowing that the ridge plus Blaven had been done previously. He did not carry water, and after breakfast at 8 a.m. did not have another drink till descending from Sgurr na h-Uamha. Blaven he reached just after sunset and descended by the long south ridge towards Camasunary. Here he was overtaken by darkness and rested for a little before continuing round the coast by the Bad Step to Loch Scavaig, then round Gars-bheinn and over the moor to Glen Brittle, which he reached just at 8.30 a.m. Only those who know that terribly rough trek from Camasunary to Glen Brittle can appreciate what it must have meant after such a tremendous day. Many parties have taken a full day for that trek alone, and not a few have been benighted on the way!

Even after such an epic feat Edwards still had surplus energy to work off. He got out the Lodge rowing-boat one morning after breakfast, rowed over the Atlantic to the Isle of Rhum, then over to Canna against wind and waves. Rain came on and visibility was poor as he started back, reaching the head of Loch Brittle about dawn, having been eighteen hours on the way.

Surely the ultimate had been reached? But no!—only two months later Sydney Thomson cut down the time for the round trip to twenty hours twenty minutes! Like Edwards he did not bother with caches or tents, though he had explored the difficult sections previously and carried more food—sandwiches, a tin of fruit, chocolates, raisins and glucose. Thomson's times were really astonishing. Not only did he cut down Bicknell's main ridge time which had stood for twelve years, but cut down by no less than seven hours the time taken by the best of the 1939 parties from Gars-bheinn to Blaven.

At the time of writing the only other person who has done the Greater Traverse is Michael Ward. The other heroes had favourable weather conditions. With Ward the weather gods hit back. He climbed Clach Glas and Blaven, joined Bill Murray in Glen Sligachan and with him traversed the ridge from north to south. Coming off Gars-bheinn a storm broke and they made for the shelter of their previously provisioned tent by Loch Coruisk. As other campers have found to their cost, storms in the valley of Coruisk are of a super variety. They were flooded out, their tent torn from its moorings and had to pack up as best they could and fight their way through the gale for many weary miles to the haven of Sligachan Inn.

Somervell, who did the main ridge thirty years ago, gained further fame with splendid efforts on Mount Everest. So it is fitting that Murray and Ward, heroes of the Greater Traverse, should follow in his footsteps and take part in the new Everest expeditions, tough climbs in the Cuillin having helped to fit them for the task.

In the light of feats as these it would be foolish to predict what cannot be done in the Cuillin. Maybe yet someone will do the Cuillin main ridge plus

99

Blaven and Clach Glas, then row across and climb the Cuillin of Rhum—all within twenty-four hours! Sydney Thomson's top-to-top time was twelve hours. Allow an hour for the ascent of Gars-bheinn, an hour for the descent from Blaven to Camasunary, thence by motor boat to Loch Scresort in Rhum, and there would be ample time left to cover the hills of Rhum within the allotted period.

The Present

THE CHARACTERS CHANGE

Up till about ten years after the 1914–18 war the pattern of Skye climbing remained much the same—practically all by members of the Scottish Mountaineering Club, the Cairngorm Club and the old-established English clubs. All increased their membership. More and more climbers came to Skye. Sligachan Hotel was enlarged in 1924, but gradually the focus was on Glen Brittle, which later became the true centre of Skye mountaineering. The Everest expedition of the 'twenties provided much publicity for mountains and mountaineering. There was an urge towards the out-of-doors. Rambling clubs of old thought in terms of day and afternoon excursions. When they extended their scope they found themselves up against the problem of accommodation. Few were campers and Highland hotels were far too expensive for the remainder.

In 1929 a group of Glasgow ramblers formed themselves into the Rucksack Club of Scotland, and built a hut to hold eight at Kinlochard and, later, another one at Arrochar. These men, now almost forgotten, were the true pioneers of the mighty Youth Hostel movement, a movement now known throughout the world and which has ninety-seven hostels and 36,000 members in Scotland alone.

The Scottish Youth Hostels Association itself was formed in 1931 and took over the two Rucksack Club huts. From the very beginning it made for the far places of Scotland and converted the little school at Glen Brittle into a rough-and-ready hostel. With a charge of a shilling a night a holiday in Skye became a possibility for those who could never have afforded it previously. Youth Hostels came into being in many other mountainous regions, and of course the young folks using them sought out the mountains.

The beginning of the Youth Hostel movement coincided with years of depression and unemployment. Far too many young men on Clydeside could not find work. The wisest and the best sought out the hills. Some of them did not bother to use the hostels. Instead they lived hard and made do with any sort of shelter—a cave, a disused bothy or even an overhanging boulder with a windbreak of stones. They had no guidance from the established mountaineering clubs, but read assiduously of mountain literature, found their own salvation and ultimately formed their own clubs.

If we regard W. W. Naismith as the father of the Scottish Mountaineering Club, then we should regard John Nimlin as the father of this new type of climber. With W. C. Dougan (killed in the war) he founded the Ptarmigan Club in 1929. Naturally the hills nearest Glasgow were the first training ground and they came to have a much more intimate knowledge of them than even the stalwarts of old. Nimlin became a supreme rock climber and magnificent leader and pioneered no less than fifteen new climbs in the Arrochar area, while hitherto unclimbable crags in Glencoe and elsewhere were sought out by him.

The climbers of old in Skye set out from Sligachan Hotel and returned to a hot bath and a four-course dinner. How different the way of the Ptarmigans on their first foray to the Cuillin! They did not even carry a tent or blankets— just arrived at Sligachan, then hunted around for a possible shelter on the moor. And such a thing is not easy to find on that desolate windswept moor. The problem was solved with the help of a rubbish dump by the roadside. From this they dug out several sheets of corrugated iron, two old wooden trestles and some tattered sacking and within half an hour built a shelter at the angle of two dykes. Heather was spread on the floor, the third wall covered with sacking and the fourth left open so that they gazed right out to the Vesuvius of Glamaig. From there they roamed the Cuillin, doing many fine climbs, often stumbling down the Basteir corrie in the late evening to cook a big dinner by candle-light over a primus. Once, too, they spent a night out, three thousand feet up, to watch the glory of the dawn over Loch Coruisk.

Other clubs followed the way of the Ptarmigans. The Creag Dhu Mountaineering Club came into being in 1930, became supreme at the art of hitch-hiking and soon ranged all over Scotland. Then in 1933 John Harvey founded the Lomond Mountaineering Club, which became the largest and the best organised of the three and which has trained hundreds in the mountain way.

These clubs were all from Clydeside, but hills were calling in other areas, the Grampian Club being formed in Dundee in 1927, the Moray Mountaineering Club in Elgin in 1931, the Corrie Club in Dundee in 1937 and the Etchachan Club in Aberdeen in 1938. Other small clubs also came into being in England, while the English university mountaineering clubs were very active in Skye.

The Cuillin became the magnet for these clubs and accommodation in Glen Brittle was taxed to the utmost during the summer months. Between Mary Campbell's and Mrs Chisholm's cottages there was only accommodation for about twenty. The Education Authority required the school, so the little hostel had to close down. Hikers had found the way to Glen Brittle and would not be denied. The demand for accommodation of the hostel type was only too evident, so the Sutherland family started an unofficial hostel of their own. This had a tiny shed with four beds and a common-room with a stove where more beds could be fitted up. It was instantly popular and Mary Campbell, not to be outdone, put up a notice at the entrance to the glen advertising "CAMPBELL'S SEASIDE HOSTEL—¼ MILE". This was an even smaller place and with Mary in charge was a very welcome haven.

Still the available accommodation could not meet the demand, and the problem was not solved till Glen Brittle Lodge was opened as a boarding-house in 1932. Long ago there was quite a village at Rhu Point four miles to the south of Glen Brittle. Ultimately the farm there was deserted and rebuilt by the Macaskills at Glen Brittle. Later a lodge was built on to it. Mr MacRae was farm manager from 1922 and became tenant in November 1931. The homely happy atmosphere which was characteristic of the other cottages became very evident at the lodge also. It instantly became popular and climbers of today remember gratefully countless kindnesses from Mr and Mrs MacRae and their sons and daughters. (No. 53.)

In the first season Dr Tom Longstaff was a distinguished visitor, while J. E. B. Wright, the well-known Lakeland mountain guide, brought large parties in June and again in August. The Abrahams came from Keswick and the Ladies' Scottish Climbing Club held a small meet. Almost every year thereafter Jerry Wright appeared with his protégés, having sometimes as many as twenty with him. Ultimately a tourist agency started all-in trips, including rock-climbing instruction and with Jerry in charge, while the Holiday Fellowship and other ramblers' associations brought many visitors.

Among the many famous mountaineers who have enjoyed hospitality at Glen Brittle Lodge are Dr Collie, Bentley Beetham, G. S. Crawford, T. A. Brocklebank, Wyn Harris, Marco Pallis (all with Himalayan experience), E. W. Hodge, H. R. C. Carr, Molly FitzGibbon and Brenda Ritchie, Graham Wilson, Dr Barlow, Graham MacPhee, J. H. B. Bell and many others.

Over these years the Climbers' Book at Sligachan shows but few entries, while that at Glen Brittle Lodge bears striking witness to the fact that the glen had become the premier centre in Skye. Many a grand climb is recorded there; again and again is there questioning of the classification of climbs in the guide-book. This is always a thorny problem when climbers foregather. On the first day of a holiday a cragsman might well find a difficult route quite severe; when he gets into form it may seem no more than moderate; while to novices some of the so-called easy routes may appear anything but, while wind, rain, snow, ice, mist make all routes harder.

Generally the descriptions are more concise than the long-winded ones of earlier days, even the main ridge traverse being dismissed in one line with only the total time given. Everyone, of course, climbs the Inaccessible sooner or later, giving rise to entries such as:

East Ridge ↑   West Ridge ↓

—all except the man who recorded:

East Ridge ↓   West Ridge ↑

and invited the comment: "Descending the Pinnacle before climbing it makes it severe."

One interesting entry reads:

"Difficult pitch in upper part of Eastern Gully Sron na Ciche (this lies up the left wall of a small cave). There is an unjustly neglected through route, which, I found, called for unusual exposure, having to remove my trousers to get through. The critical chest or hip measurements appear to be about 36 inches. There is no technical difficulty—except for mixed parties."

The Present

The inevitable comment appeared in verse:

ON READING THE ABOVE

To this land of ancient heroes,
Mountain, stream, and rugged hill,
Came an English youth who showed that
Dauntless men are with us still.

Hied he off to Sron na Ciche
Did that lad of Saxon race,
To surmount the long steep gully
Cleaving straight its eastern face.

Climbed he steadily and surely,
Till at last he reached a cave,
High upon that rugged mountain:
Surely this would test the brave.

"Clear the way does lie before me,
I must go straight up and through."
Of the perils of the venture
And its risks—ah, well he knew!

"Is it possible?" he wonders.
"Show me how," he now supplants,
Till a light dawns in the darkness;
"Bravo, I'll remove my pants."

And the Goddess of the Mountain,
Who observes the climber's play,
Could scarce conceal her admiration
As she coyly turned away.

Sing no more of Smythe and Odell,
Give your Everest man a miss:
Epic climbs they've made, we grant you,
But never in a state like this.

Everyone sang the praises of Glen Brittle, and one described it intriguingly as "a semi-virgin rock-climbers' Paradise".

The Soay fishermen brought their motor boat over to Loch Brittle and soon there was a regular service to the Isle of Soay and Loch Scavaig, with time ashore to visit Loch Coruisk, while parties could arrange for longer trips to Rhum, Eigg, or Canna. For an off day from the mountains such trips are ideal, while a sailing-cum-climbing expedition became very popular. The party would visit Soay, go on to Loch Scavaig, picnic by Loch Coruisk and return to Glen Brittle over the ridge of the Dubhs and the Thearlaich-Dubh gap.

Not always did everything go to schedule. A sudden storm forced one party to stay overnight on Soay, where they were hospitably entertained by the MacDonalds with a ceilidh for their benefit. There are other tales of incredible wanderings in thick mist on the crags above Coir' a' Ghrunnda, and of climbers descending on the wrong side of the ridge to find themselves, towards evening, back at Loch Coruisk and forced to make a long weary journey in darkness round the base of the hills.

Sea-mountaineering started. Thirty years previously large private steam yachts had brought tourists to Portree Bay, thence to Sligachan. Now small motor craft brought climbers to Glen Brittle. E. W. Hodge's parties, in several trips, visited almost every island of the Hebrides and usually climbed to the highest part of it. The very names of the places visited arouse envy in the hearts of less fortunate mortals:

"From Greenock to Eigg, Rhum, Canna, Loch Nevis, Loch Brittle."
"From Rhu via Iona, Staffa, Castlebay, Eriskay, Rodil, St Kilda, Loch Brittle."
"From Rhu via Jura, Garvelloch Isles, Lunga, Castlebay, Rhum, South Rona, North Harris, St Kilda, Loch Scavaig, Loch Brittle."

Camping increased. Tents were pitched by the shoreside, by the river and in the corries. Not once but many times washed-out campers were to be found in MacRae's barn. Adventurous motorists even towed trailer caravans over from Carbost, and those who know that awful rutted road will realise their daring.

Colin Kirkus, that supreme leader, whose feats in Snowdonia had astonished even the experts, was one of the campers of this period. As happened with many another "tiger", he was tamed by the magnificence of the Cuillin and the glory of the ridges. Alf Bridge, his companion, relates how they were so supremely happy that they did not even think of new routes, and quotes a

106

remark of Colin's on the summit of Sgurr Alasdair: "You know, Alf, going to the right place, at the right time, with the right people is *all* that really matters. What one does is purely incidental."

The influx of campers and hostellers created a problem of supplies, for the nearest shop is eight miles away. This was solved by the Carbost grocer bringing his van over twice a week. He ran it up on to the field where most of the tents were to be found, thus bringing a shop to the campers' doorstep.

Aeroplanes also reached Glen Brittle. One could leave Renfrew at 9.30 a.m. and land at Glen Brittle at 11 a.m., contrasting with the twelve-hour journey by rail, sea and road. Often from our camp we watched the plane circling round above and land on that flat field between Glen Brittle Lodge and the sea. The service was carried on with the utmost regularity and there was never an accident. But there was no other suitable field in the island and the terrible state of the road out of the glen ultimately led to the withdrawal of the service.

When one remembers that the Cuillin are the most difficult peaks in Britain there had been remarkably few accidents among them up till this time. Nor is there any record of any of the pioneer climbers coming to grief on these hills. These men encountered far more loose rock than is met with by the climbers of today. They knew their business and climbed safely A newcomer was usually introduced to the Cuillin by an experienced climber, while tourists stuck to certain routes and were often with guides. During the period 1870–1930 there were but three fatalities and all to inexperienced parties.

The great increase in the number of visitors inevitably led to more accidents. Five of the six accidents in the 1930–40 period were to novice climbers or tourists, due usually to a lack of normal precautions. One affair in 1935 was reminiscent of the Greg accident of 1893, but the tourists, lacking the experience of Mr Greg, did not win through. Wearing unnailed shoes, and with no knowledge of the hills, they left Elgol, telling no one of their plans. A day or two later the body of one of them was found in the Visigill burn near Carbost. Months afterwards a second body was found in Coire na Creiche. Apparently they had gone from Elgol to Coruisk, crossed the range at Bealach na Glaic Moire and come to grief on the descent. Mr Greg's descent had been somewhat similar, but he knew the lie of the land and made for the Carbost road. When one of these tourists collapsed, the other continued, crossed the Bealach a' Mhaim path (just as Mr Greg did), but wandered for three miles parallel to the road, the body being found quite near it. They had tried an expedition well beyond their powers and had paid the penalty.

This affair received wide publicity in the press and was followed by articles suggesting prohibition of climbing among such dangerous peaks. Since the days of Whymper there has been something inherently dramatic about mountain accidents, so that they receive much more publicity than they deserve. A motoring fatality may only get a few lines, a mountain accident a column, sometimes a page, thus giving rather a false impression of danger. The press, however, are never able to distinguish between climbers and tourists. Than rock climbing there is no sport so misunderstood by outsiders. No one believes that a steeplejack on a high chimney is in danger, because they know he is on a ladder with good holds and knows his job. So is the climber safe high up on the cliff, for he too knows his job and the holds are there. The holds are of all sizes and types and their proper use is not easily learned. To the outsider a cliff face is that and nothing more; to the climber it is a place of infinite variety—with ledges, gullies, cracks and chimneys—and with careful technique he can ascend with absolute safety. And all the time he can feel safe, which means more. In sixty years of climbing among the Cuillin no member of the Scottish Mountaineering Club has lost his life, while the old-established English clubs have a similar record. For the inexperienced danger ever lurks.

The greater number, however, learned the way of the mountains and were able to look after themselves. Whereas mountaineering formerly had been the sport of a select few, now it had become a sport for all. Though new climbs were but few, the numbers who won health and pleasure and inspiration from the Cuillin increased a hundredfold. Climbing was at last taking its place in the scheme of things

The rush to Glen Brittle was but an echo of the tourist traffic throughout Skye generally. Barns became garages. Bus services covered every road bar that awful road to Glen Brittle. Even the much enlarged Sligachan Hotel could scarce cope with the demand for accommodation. While Glen Brittle was almost the preserve of the climber, tourists, fishermen *and* climbers flocked to Sligachan. Harry Lauder came and from his verses—

> *The hills are bare and bonny,*
> *The road is lang and steep,*
> *But the air is saft and balmy:*
> *Skye's the place to sleep.*

—we may assume he, at least, did not climb Sgurr nan Gillean.

H. V. Morton in *In Search of Scotland* called the name Cuillin " piffling ",

53. Glen Brittle House and the South Cuillin

54. Mrs Chisholm, hostess of climbers. Her little post office on the far side of the River Brittle has been a climbers' haven since 1912

59. Loch an Fhir-Bhallaich—many of one's brightest memories of the Cuillin
are of bathing in cool mountain lochans such as this

60. Evening shadows on the Cuillin with the climbers G. A. Marskell, W. H. Murray and
Kenneth Dunn, reluctant to leave the heights. They are on the summit of Sgurr a'
Ghreadaidh with Sgurr Alasdair and Sgurr Dearg in the background

61. On the summit of Sgurr Alasdair looking north. The Inaccessible Pinnacle can be seen over-topping Sgurr Dearg and beyond it are Sgurr na Banadich, Sgurr Thormaid and Sgurr a' Ghreadaidh with Sgurr Thuilm faintly seen in the background

62. W. H. Murray near the top of the East Gully of Sron na Ciche with an unusual view of A'Chioch far below

but I imagine he did not see much of them, as he did not climb any of the great peaks. The Cuillin is no piffling name. When pronounced, not as a Sassenach pronounces it, but with that lovable inflexion only the Highlander can give, it is a very splendid name—the only possible name.

From all the airts they came. Elizabeth Knowlton came from the U.S.A. and afterwards wrote a glowing account of the Cuillin for the *American Alpine Journal,* while even Soviet climbers enjoyed themselves on Sron na Ciche.

One climber brought with him two Swiss guides. The Cuillin greatly impressed those experts from the Alps, though they could never understand how so much sea could be around so much climbing. Others returned when they could do no more than gaze up at the great peaks, and F. C. Digby records:

"Came here first in 1873, met Sheriff Nicolson and Angus MacPherson the Guide, then in 1887 with H. Walker and C. Pilkington climbed the Inaccessible Pinnacle of Sgurr Dearg—lost on Blaven—returned in my 80th year to revisit the scenes of my youth in this delightful island."

ONE MAN'S TREASURE

A book such as this must inevitably deal with the great figures of our sport, those bold spirits who seek out new climbs and venture on untrodden rock. Yet the vast number of climbers do not seek to be the first to pass; the climbing and the mountains count more than the actual climb. It is the fascination of the Cuillin that they hold untold delights for such as these. The story of the tigers has already been told; that be the excuse for the story of one of the most ordinary of climbers.

For me, one of the special delights of Glen Brittle lies in the number and variety of its approaches. There is the classic route over the Bealach a' Mhaim from Sligachan, the prosaic route by road from Carbost, the lonely route over the moors from Loch Eynort, the toughest route round the coast from Elgol and the adventurous route by small craft from Mallaig. I have tried them all and only regret I never had the pleasure of reaching Glen Brittle by air.

Graven indelibly in my memory is my first glimpse of that glen. George MacKay and I had started from Kyleakin and spent ten days walking round the north part of Skye, leaving the Cuillin till the very end. Often we saw them from afar, from Portree, from the summit of the Storr, and, when walking southwards, the mist would lift to reveal their splintered peaks.

Our route to Glen Brittle was one seldom used—by road from Carbost to lonely Loch Eynort, then over the moor where the map shows a track which we never found. We crossed a low col and Glen Brittle lay before us—a green glen, a house or two, a shining stretch of sand, waves dancing in sunshine and in the background the whole magnificent range of the South Cuillin. Even yet I think that these little easy hills on the west side of Loch Brittle are just about the finest viewpoint for the Cuillin.

Not knowing that a bridge existed we waded across the River Brittle to reach the road on the far side, and when we enquired for accommodation were directed to Mrs Chisholm's cottage. How fortunate we were! She had a room vacant and took us in. Casual trampers would never now find accommodation at Glen Brittle during the Glasgow Fair week.

It was early afternoon. There were the Cuillin. We had to go for a climb though we knew nothing about them. We were well up on Sgurr Dearg when mist came down and hunger sent us back to the haven of Mrs Chisholm's and her incomparable cooking.

Next day dawned clear. Remembering John Mackenzie's statement that Sgurr Alasdair was "just a walk" we made our way up into Coire Lagan and managed to identify the Great Stone Shoot. That "easy way" has been much maligned, but taken slowly it forms a highway to the main ridge even for complete novices. It was thrilling to reach the top of the Shoot and gaze down on Coir' a' Ghrunnda on the far side, even more thrilling to climb the short remaining section to the highest point in Skye. For ten days the summit of Sgurr Alasdair had been our goal—now it was ours!

The whole range of the Cuillin was around us, though we were then only able to identify a few of the peaks, such as the Inaccessible Pinnacle and Blaven.

Another thrill came when we first saw rock climbers in action. Two men appeared on the narrow crest of the Sgumain ridge and came slowly towards us. Then they disappeared on the steeper section below, till, later, the leader's head appeared at our feet. After telling us they were "doing the round of Coire Lagan" they moved on. The phrase meant nothing to us. Now it is redolent of the very best of Cuillin memories.

For an hour we stayed on the summit in brilliant sunshine, then MacKay scared me by insisting that we return by a different route, while I, ever cautious, thought we had better go back the way we had come. I should explain here that I was wearing boots with a few hobnails, while he had ordinary walking shoes with rubber soles, and both of us wore shorts.

We followed the ridge a short distance towards Sgurr Sgumain then descended direct to Lochan Coir' a' Ghrunnda. That descent is just a confused memory to me and we were lucky to get down safely. It was only when we found a copy of the S.M.C. Guide to Skye at Mrs Chisholm's that evening that we learned of the existence of a mountaineering club in Scotland and appreciated how foolish we were. We could not locate our route among the Ghrunnda face climbs described in the Guide and, though I have been in Coir' a' Ghrunnda many times since then, I have not been able to pick it out. Most certainly it is not a route for unroped novices and beginner's luck must have been with us.

Of that holiday such was our only climb in the Cuillin. George MacKay had the makings of a first-rate rock climber. He chose matrimony and an anxious wife instead and never climbed again.

Climbing became all in all to me during the years which followed. Before I climbed among the Cuillin again I ascended all the lesser hills of Skye alone. This included the Broadford group of hills, Marsco and Glamaig, the Storr and Beinn Edra and the flat-topped hills known as MacLeod's Tables. Many go direct to the Cuillin on a first holiday in Skye, but I do not regret those 'prentice days on the lesser hills.

Once I tried to take a very ancient car all the way to Glen Brittle. After a complete breakdown on the Mallaig road I left it behind me and continued by train, ferry and bus to Sligachan. At 9.30 p.m. I started over the Bealach a' Mhaim with a 50-lb. load. I had left home at 5 a.m. and was very tired. Every time I sat down to rest I fell off to sleep—and I sat down very often.

About midnight I reached the road, lay down in the heather and slept for an hour before continuing to Glen Brittle. My friends were camping there but I did not wish to disturb anyone in the middle of the night and, being too tired to pitch my own tent, just spread out my waterproof sheet halfway between two encampments, got into my sleeping bag and fell off to sleep at once.

A moment or two later—though it was really hours—I was awakened by something tugging at the end of my sleeping bag. Without opening my eyes I knew it was daylight and thought my friends had found me and were having a game. I kept quiet till the tugs became vicious. I opened my eyes. A big white horse was chewing at the end of my sleeping bag—and my feet were inside! I shooed it away. No good! The colour seemed to attract it and it always returned. I got up and ran to the nearest tent. It was empty. I grabbed my kit, bundled everything in and went off to sleep again, too tired to puzzle over the problem of the empty tent (it was 5 a.m.) but not too tired to note from stray garments that it was obviously a woman's tent. Later I discovered that its owner had gone up to Coire Lagan to see the sunrise.

Of many holidays in Skye, one stands out beyond all others. Come with me to Skye in June—the best month of all the year. At four o'clock on a Friday evening Ian Maitland and I left Glasgow, the car loaded to the roof and the weather set fair. I had been climbing at least every second weekend since the beginning of the year and always in the West Highlands, so that almost every mountain had its own memories.

Looking back from Tyndrum the Crianlarich mountains were fairer than I had ever seen them—that dusky blue colour which is the forerunner of good weather. On we sped over the Black Mount road, to be welcomed in Glencoe by Buchaille Etive Mor, now bright and sunny and contrasting strongly with the dark and glowering mountain where rain had washed out our camp a few weeks previously. Nearing Clachaig, just a glimpse of the twin summit buttresses of Bidein nam Bian, the highest peak in Argyllshire, then on to Ballachullish ferry, from where Gars-bheinn of Ardgour appeared dim and dreamy in a heat haze. Now by Loch Linnhe and through Fort William; beyond the town that magnificent view of Allt a' Mhuillin with the ridges of Ben Nevis showing up clearly.

Crossing from Spean Bridge to Inverlochy, the whole moorland was alive with colour, acres and acres of rhododendron, then a blaze of gorse. Only when we crossed the Great Glen were we truly on "The Road to the Isles", and while I think the route from Fort William to Mallaig the finer of the alternative train journeys, I place that by Glen Garry as the finest for a car. By the quiet Loch Garry grand old fir trees were reflected in its clear waters. We passed a car facing south and saw some climbers sitting by the lochside. "Poor devils," we thought—probably *returning* from Skye and reluctant to go back to civilisation on such a wondrous night.

From Tomdoun a hill road led us over to Cluanie and soon we sighted the peaks of Kintail. Then a rush down Glen Shiel with the peak of the Saddle dominating the scene. Up again, up and up, by the twisting Mam Ratagan road. It was nearing sunset now and we could look over the feathery tops of the nearer fir trees to Loch Duich lying far below with the Five Sisters of Kintail beyond.

Then downhill through Glenelg and on to the ferry. It was 10.30 p.m. All was quiet. We saw no one, yet by the shoreside was a brazier of coals glowing faintly. We questioned not the reason, just pumped at the bellows and had soup heating up in a couple of minutes. Maybe the wee folk in green had arranged all this knowing we would be too late for the ferry?

On a little headland above the ferry slip we found a perfect place to spend the night—a sheltered hollow of deep luxurious heather twenty feet above the sea and within half a mile of Skye. Soon we were snug. At 4.30 a.m. I woke up to a spatter of rain, pulled the oilskins over and went to sleep again. What did it matter? Soon we would be in Skye!

When the workmen repairing the ferry slip arrived at 8 a.m. they found their brazier already in use—to cook our breakfast. We crossed by the first ferry, remembering that this was the route Samuel Johnson took on the famous journey. We did not dally, like him, at Broadford but rushed on to Sligachan where the Cuillin were awaiting us.

A training walk being indicated after so much motoring, we climbed Sgurr nan Gillean by the tourist route. Even if classified as such it is always interesting to follow the route by which a great mountain was first climbed, and this way has the merit that the tourist does not see anything of the Cuillin till he reaches the actual ridge and then the whole wild immensity of them bursts into view. And that section from the ridge to the summit of Sgurr nan Gillean is harder for the tourist than many of the other less known Cuillin peaks. But perhaps the shattered West Ridge, like a jerry-built wall, makes many tourists decide that Sgurr nan Gillean will be their first and last Cuillin peak.

The best part of that day was a bathe in a crystal clear pool in the Red Burn on the way back to Sligachan. Just as we were leaving the hotel a car drove up and an old man stepped out. Tall he was and upright, a notable figure in any company and that nose was unmistakable. It was Professor Collie! So was our holiday blessed with a glimpse of the greatest Cuillin climber of them all.

Less pleasant was the sad encounter with a lamb on the road to Drynoch which led to its demise. We met the shepherd, asked him its value and paid in full. Having paid for the lamb I wanted to take it with us, but Ian would not agree. He doubted our ability to cook it over a primus stove, and anyway, he said, we had no mint sauce.

113

The Cuillin of Skye

In Glen Brittle we found Bill Murray's party camping at a fine site by the river and soon had our tent up nearby. Our warm welcome was mainly because we carried a goodly supply of oil of citronella with which to fight the midges—the curse of Skye. That oil is an efficient preventive in most places, but the Skye midges seemed to feed on it, then started to feed on us. Midges were everywhere. We ate boiled midges, fried midges, stewed midges and drowned midges! Not till after the war and the appearance of the newer midge-preventives was the curse really removed.

We thought we had done well by leaving Glasgow at 4 p.m. and reaching Glenelg at 10.30 p.m., but MacAlpine, a rock-climbing novice on his first visit to Skye, had left town about the same time, motored to Mallaig, crossed by car ferry to Armadale and reached Glen Brittle by midnight. Not content with that, he went off at once with Murray and was on the top of the Cioch within twelve hours of leaving Glasgow.

Next day the heat wave turned on and remained with us for the rest of our stay. Almost every journey up to Coire Lagan meant a bathe in Loch an Fhirbhallaich and another in Lochan Coire Lagan. Hence progress was usually very slow. On the first day we managed up Sgurr Sgumain and along the ridge over Sgurr Alasdair to Sgurr Thearlaich. Hereabouts I found a Fair Isle sweater. I recognised it at once as belonging to Douglas Scott, for many a time I had followed it on a rock climb. He and Rob Anderson had left Glen Brittle at 10 p.m. three days previously to do the main ridge. Leaving a sweater was clear evidence of the heat they experienced. Ultimately they preferred the cool waters in Coir' a' Ghreadaidh to being parboiled on the ridge. So was it also with us. The lochan below and a cooling swim called more loudly than the next peak, Sgurr Mhic Coinnich. In the morning the cliffs of Sron na Ciche had been in shadow; now every detail showed up, with the shadow of the Cioch very clear. It must have been the same time of the evening that Collie first discovered the Cioch fifty years ago, as his photograph of the cliffs is much the same as mine. (No. 32.)

The others went off to camp while I climbed Sgurr Alasdair once more to see the sunset. At 9 p.m. the whole range of the Cuillin were in shadow and quite dark, with the Red Hills and Blaven quite clear and beyond the faint outline of the Kintail peaks, a rosy haze above them fading into a light blue sky. The sun was now sinking just over Neist Point with its last rays lighting up Loch Bracadale and silhouetting MacLeod's Maidens. In the afternoon there had been many parties on the ridges; now I seemed to have the whole range

114

to myself. Had I not been expected back at camp I would surely have stayed on Sgurr Alasdair all night.

Time matters little in Skye in June, for darkness exists only for an hour or so. One may climb at any time of the day or night. The usual programme was a long substantial breakfast and seldom were we off before 11 a.m., returning eight to twelve hours later according to the state of our appetite. One day it would be the Window Buttress and the Inaccessible, another the ridges north of Sgurr na Banachdich or the rock-climbing playground of Sron na Ciche. Variety is endless and days may be easy or strenuous. The photographs (Nos. 67, 68) were taken after Bill and I had climbed the Inaccessible by the steep western side, descended by the east ridge and returned to the foot of the steep side to retrieve our packs. A couple then appeared on the summit and the man let the lady down, then hitched his rope round a spike and slid down quickly. Alas, he had used the wrong belay! The rope would not come off and he had to climb up once more, transfer it to the proper belay and slide down again.

Of the ridge walks in Skye I shall always prefer the traverse of the five peaks which circle round Coire Lagan. In such weather our round was a most leisurely one, involving hours of bathing in the lochans on the way up and countless stops for photography. It was one o'clock before we reached the summit of the Cioch, but what a perfect place for lunch, while the others posed obligingly for photographs. The East Gully led us to the summit ridge, and the appearance of the Cioch from the top of it is well shown in the photograph (No. 62).

Then one works slowly round—Sgurr Sgumain, Sgurr Alasdair, Sgurr Thearlaich, to enjoy a bit of harder rock climbing in King's Chimney of Sgurr Mhic Coinnich. Just uncouth names to the Philistines, a thousand delights to the devout. We must have made a record for slowness that day, for I remember as I neared the top of the long side of the Inaccessible an orb of bronze suddenly came into view; the sun was sinking in the west.

No climbing holiday in Skye is complete without a night out. Bill Murray had been climbing for ten days, yet had never visited Loch Coruisk. I knew it of old and had always wanted to reach it from the mountains in the early morning. Thus we started off from camp at 10.30 p.m. one night and made up Coire na Banachdich. For the first time we encountered mist and it became darker than usual. At midnight I had a bathe in a shallow pool at the highest point of the burn, while Murray sat and smoked. In the growing darkness we had to go cautiously as we zigzagged upwards over broken rock. At 12.40 a.m.

we arrived at a sloping ledge with a rock wall on one side and an impressive drop below. There was no need to speak. We just donned extra sweaters and lay down. Normally we would have seen the glen and our camp; the mist and darkness made us feel much more among the mountains. It was quite calm and not at all cold. I dozed, dreamed and planned, then dropped off to sleep. So passed the darkest hours.

At 2 a.m. we awoke and moved off at once. There was thick mist around and rock to negotiate; with sleep not yet out of our eyes we had to tread carefully. Soon we reached the main ridge, and it was an eerie business finding our way along it in the grey ghostly hours before the dawn. Rock towers loomed up out of the mist and were climbed or turned. The scratches of hundreds of hobnailed boots showed the way unmistakably.

On, over the two tops of Sgurr na Banachdich, with clumps of starry saxifrage near each cairn, on over Sgurr Thormaid to Sgurr a' Ghreadaidh. I commiserated with Murray that, on this, our long excursion, we should see nothing but mist. He grunted and pointed to the south. It was strangely light now. We were among clouds, not mist! Away to the south a sharp cone of rock appeared. That was but the beginning, and the wonder of it all is still with me. The clouds sank slowly. Peak after peak came into view as if to greet the dawn. It was fascinating and not at all easy to pick them out and name them when detached from their connecting ridges and divorced from their corries. North of us was Sgurr nan Gillean, and the sun, though hidden in clouds, was rising above it, tinging the outline of the mountain with a rosy light. As the clouds sank lower we could trace the whole serrated ridge from north to south. The clouds moved continuously. Great masses of them rolled over the bealach between Bidein Druim nan Ramh and Sgurr a' Mhadaidh and poured themselves down to the abyss where lay Coruisk. On the other side of the ridge clouds stretched away to the far distance, so that the peaks were like crags rising from an arctic ice-field.

Suddenly a tremendous peak appeared in the east. It could only be "Blaven, mighty Blaven", a very Everest that morning. Photography was not easy, for a short time-exposure was necessary and I had no tripod. By resting the camera on the rock I managed to capture something of the effect (No. 64). After that I went off to sleep. When I woke up, Bill was sound asleep and within a foot or so of a considerable drop to the corrie below. Thought I, "One good roll, my lad, and you'll be well on your way to Coruisk." Fortunately he stayed put, so that I was able to photograph him before waking him up.

116

The Present

At 7 a.m. in bright sunshine we moved on over the four rock tops of Sgurr a' Mhadaidh. Still the clouds swirled below us; from camp they saw nothing but mist at a thousand feet, so that the cloud layer would be a thousand to fifteen hundred feet thick.

The great heroes who do the Cuillin main ridge in a day take just about one hour from Sgurr na Banachdich to Sgurr a' Mhadaidh. We took six hours and are not ashamed. Haste would have been sacrilege that morning.

At 9 a.m. we started downwards from Bealach na Glaic Moire. The gods were kind. As we descended so did the mist and clouds disappear and for the rest of the day all peaks were clear. Had the early visitors seen Loch Coruisk as we saw it they would never have penned such gloomy descriptions as "grim and awesome", "perpetual darkness". All was bright and welcoming that summer day and we had the bathe of a lifetime in a transparent green-blue pool where the river enters the loch. Nor did early visitors stop to notice the flowers. The ling, the true Scottish heather, was only in bud, but the bell heather was in full bloom. We trod through ferns and young bracken. We saw wild roses, a thicket of hazel and a solitary rowan tree; brambles tore our legs, the sundew flower glinted in the bogs and butterwort and dog violet grew in profusion.

Our arrival was well timed. We had the loch to ourselves for an hour or two, then MacBrayne's *Loch Ness* steamed into Loch Scavaig and dropped anchor. A ship! Passengers! Food! An obliging boatman took us out and we caused something of a sensation as we drew up at the side of the ship. Bill had a straggling growth of a week's duration on his face; I was not much better, while the adhesive gabbro had claimed a good deal of my trousers. The passengers, Scottish, English, American, were lined up waiting to go ashore and we had to pass them all. Nothing mattered but food! The steward rose to the occasion nobly. We had only twenty minutes and in that time had an excellent lunch—soup, fish, roast lamb and mint sauce with lots of salad, two big helpings—toast, bread, butter, jam and as many cups of coffee as we could drink. Before that feed we had given up the idea of "doing the Dubhs". Now we were ready for anything.

Back ashore and how different Coruisk! Tourists were scattered all over the southern shores of the loch. Some never managed that stony half-mile of path from Loch Scavaig, while others were staggering along on high-heeled shoes. Wild men of the mountains they took us for and we had to run the gauntlet of their cameras.

117

The Cuillin of Skye

At four o'clock we started up the glaciated slabs of Sgurr Dubh Beag. The slabs are inclined like the roof of a house and would be quite impossible on most rock formations other than the blessed gabbro. The weather was tropical now and that eastern ridge was sheer delight. Far below lay Coruisk with gulls wheeling around its islands. Beyond were the lighter waters of Scavaig, the green Isle of Soay and laughing summer seas extending out to the cloud-shadowed Cuillin of Rhum. (No. 66.)

The summit at last, a drop to the bealach, the only place where we used the rope all day, then on to Sgurr Dubh Mor. But how we suffered from thirst! What took me up that mountain was the thought of the tin of grapefuit we would enjoy at its top. Every particle of it I consumed slowly, rolling it round my mouth to savour the full relish of it and moisten my parched throat. The Sgurr Alasdair group of peaks looked quite near and we could trace our route of the early morning—blue skies, blue seas, the Cuillin at their very finest.

So refreshed we moved on to Sgurr Dubh na Da Bheinn. What now? It was nine o'clock and we had told camp we would be back within twenty-four hours. So we had to give up the idea of crossing the Thearlaich gap to Coire Lagan, as we would not have appreciated it properly at that time of night and when feeling rather tired. Instead, we rushed down to Loch Coir' a' Ghrunnda, had a last meal there—sardines—then a fast walk over the moor took us back to camp exactly at 10.30 p.m. Bill agreed I had shown him the best route to Coruisk.

Not even midges would have prevented a sound sleep that night. I wakened to someone pushing in porridge and bacon and egg at 10.30 a.m. and went off to sleep again. It was my first day off and I was content just to gaze up at the mountains which had captured me so completely. Wisps of cloud touched the summits and the sun as hot as ever. Towards evening the Cuillin stood out clearly in sunshine, with every ridge and gully showing up, and, through the glasses, I could see a party on the Cioch and another on the summit of Sgurr Alasdair.

No holiday is complete without a motor-boat trip. The MacDonalds collected us and took us over to Soay, where we had time to explore that little island. The houses are substantial and I noted far better vegetable gardens than on the mainland of Skye. The Islefolk of Soay have been good friends to climbers and the climbers, by making increasing use of their boats, have helped the Islefolk. Surely evacuation is not necessary?

From Soay we went over to Loch Scavaig, picnicked by Coruisk, where the gulls, tourist-conscious and tourist-fed, are almost tame. It was a lovely lazy day, yet my diary notes regret I had not gone for the peaks. Such is always the way in the younger, eager days.

Sometimes we were very late in making for the hills. One morning we seemed quite unable to climb, perhaps because of the big breakfast we had consumed and which consisted of generous helpings of porridge, fruit pudding, kippers, bacon and eggs, tea, bread, Ryvita, jam, honey and so on. It was after six o'clock at night before we left camp for a farewell to the Cioch. Mist was low down in Coire Lagan and things did not promise well. The Cuillin had yet another surprise for us. As we climbed up we found ourselves emerging from dense, dirty mist on to the top of lovely white clouds with a normal sky-scape above and the sun sinking in the west. The tip of the Cioch rose in sun-shine above the cloud level, which stretched out for many miles.

If there be such a thing as photographic ecstasy I knew it that night. If I could capture that effect it would be the photograph of a lifetime. I posed Bill on the summit, unroped, and climbed quickly along the knife-edge ridge to get a stance. I had no tripod, no lens hood, no exposure meter. It was after 9 p.m. and the photo had to be taken dead against the sun. There was but one thing to do—to expose for the clouds and leave the rock in silhouette. I held the camera upside down so that the extending baseboard acted as a lens hood and took three photographs in rapid succession, each at 1/50 second, but varying the aperture, and of course I had a filter permanently fitted behind the lens. The photograph (No. 69) was the result.

THE WAR AND AFTER

In pre-war time mountaineering was often derided as a foolhardy pastime. When the need came for men to lead the attack on the Hitlerite fortress of Europe it was realised that the training of the mountaineers was essential. Thus came into being the Commandos and Mountain Warfare Training. Rigorous training was carried out in the Cairngorms, the West Highlands and in North Wales.

In the summer of 1941 troops first stormed the Cuillin of Skye. E. A. M. Wedderburn was in charge and a week in Skye was the finale of a three weeks' course which started in Glencoe. The general idea was to train men to climb routes up to difficult standard, while carrying military equipment.

The Cuillin of Skye

In November and December of that year a larger party under T. M. Wedderburn were in Skye. To get accommodation for eighty officers and men was not easy, so they were spread out from Luib to Glen Brittle with headquarters at Sligachan. In spite of bad weather—there were only two days when the Cuillin were clear of mist—much fine climbing was done. It is to be regretted that no photographs are available of armed soldiers traversing the classic Pinnacle Ridge of Sgurr nan Gillean. Other climbs done were the North Face of Am Basteir, the Window Buttress and the Inaccessible Pinnacle of Sgurr Dearg, Collie's route on Sgurr Alasdair and many ascents on Sron na Ciche, including Eastern Buttress, Cioch Gully, Cioch West and Cioch Upper Buttress. Thus were introduced to the Cuillin many who would never have gone near them. Generally the men rapidly grasped the elements of rock-climbing technique and progress was often astonishing.

In the following year there was a mock invasion with Commandos landing at Camasunary and Loch Scavaig and attacking Sligachan where Home Guard units were stationed, but there was no further organised rock-climbing training.

Climbers in the forces occasionally spent their leave in Skye. For others, as the island was in "protected area", Skye was but a dream all during the dreary war years.

With the arrival of peace there was a great surge towards the out-of-doors and the mountains. Many new clubs were formed, the tendency being for small groups such as those of Carlisle, Preston, Greenock, Forfar, Stirling and many other places. Almost every college and university in Britain soon had its mountaineering club, while it was significant that it was left to a small Yorkshire club to bring out a rock-climbing guide to the remote Island of Rhum.

Skye was once more the magnet. One of the younger mountaineering clubs, the Moray Club from Elgin, brought a party of forty. They all travelled by bus and erected their own marquee beside a cottage of which they had the use. By doing all their own cooking the total cost of transport and all food for a long weekend was no more than £2 a head.

Glen Brittle was ready with a fine new Youth Hostel with accommodation for ninety, the Lodge and the well-known cottages of old. With campers added the climbing population could be numbered in hundreds, compared with dozens of former years.

In 1942, during convalescence after an illness, I tried to get to Skye and wrote Mrs Chisholm, who replied that the Cuillin were in grand condition with no one to climb them. A permit did not come through, so I promised myself the Cuillin the first summer after the war.

After such a long absence the approach to Glen Brittle had to be a novel one —by motor-boat from Mallaig. I travelled north the day previously and spent the night at Morar. So stormy was it that we could not even go fishing on the in-land Loch Morar, while next morning the Sound of Sleat was a mass of white-caps. It looked as if we would have to take the prosaic route by ferry and bus.

Sandy, our fisherman, reassured us. Of course he would take all twelve of us to Loch Brittle! Once out of the sheltered harbour we met Atlantic seas; now and then huge combers broke over and drenched the unlucky ones, but ours was a grand sea boat and held steadily on. Bright blue skies, masses of cumulus clouds, behind us the grape-black peaks of Knoydart and Kintail, on the port the white sands of Morar, ahead the Scuir of Eigg challenging the seas and the Cuillin of Rhum standing out majestically.

Only Tom MacKinnon, John Nimlin and myself kept our dinners; all the rest were dead sick. Never did I believe that faces could actually look green till I saw the results of a ciné film in colour taken during that voyage.

Towards the Point of Sleat the waves became bigger and the seas rougher. Sandy, a tough old pirate, took us cannily round. Now the wind was behind us; with huge following seas we swept in towards the Cuillin. Was there ever such an approach as this? There was the huge mass of Blaven. Coruisk lay in that dark hollow. There was the whole range of the Cuillin, splintered peak upon splintered peak, coming nearer every moment.

Confused seas again as we rounded Rudha an Dunain into the home waters of Loch Brittle. The invalids had all recovered by this time and the old hands were busy pointing out and naming all the peaks to them. Ahead of us was the grandest of all Cuillin corries, Coire Lagan, the hoary peaks around it a climbers' litany—Sgumain, Alasdair, Thearlaich, Mhic Coinnich and Dearg.

At nine o'clock at night, after a seven instead of the expected four hours' sail we landed by the River Brittle. Mrs Chisholm's, Mary Campbell's and Glen Brittle House were full up. Some of us got into the Youth Hostel, the remainder into Sutherland's unofficial one. Next day, the rope, the hobnailed boots, the fingers tingling to the rasp of the gabbro—a Cuillin climb once more, and surely ours was the perfect return to the glen.

The Window Buttress of Sgurr Dearg and the Inaccessible was the chosen climb for our first day. I remember best watching the ladies of the Lomonds descending the steep side of the Inaccessible with grace and celerity.

John and Jenny Nimlin were introducing their daughter to the Cuillin, and we carried her up to Coire Lagan, discovering that a two-year-old kiddie can be quite a weight on the shoulders! We picnicked by that lovely little lochan, and when rain threatened started to make a howff—a windbreak of stones against an overhanging boulder. With one rucksack for a pillow, her feet shoved into another, the kiddie was placed inside and went off to sleep. Her father and mother then made for a climb on the Cioch, leaving me to look after the baby. Dorothy, fortunately, was used to this sort of thing, as she had camped out since she was three months old. She gave no trouble, so that I was able to spend the time collecting and identifying all the flowers in the upper corrie. To the casual glance there appears to be nothing but grey rock, boulders and scree. On the far side of the lochan, at a height of about nineteen hundred feet, there is sparse greenery with minute flowers one might well walk over without noticing. I noted clumps of rose root, carpets of wild thyme, Alpine ladies'-mantle, lots of tormentil, bog asphodel, dog violet and common butterwort, together with various saxifrages, still another proof that count-less writers have erred in denying the Cuillin any vegetation.

Our day was not destined to end so happily. Scarcely had John and Jenny returned when a climber came towards us from the direction of the Sgurr Alasdair Stone Shoot, his very appearance indicating that something was seriously wrong. He explained that he and his companion, a Polish soldier, had been traversing Sgurr Mhic Coinnich unroped when a loose stone was dis-lodged. This hit the Pole, who was knocked off his balance and fell away down out of sight on the Coruisk side. From the account given, and our knowledge of the ground, we were of the opinion that the Pole must have been killed, but this fact had to be ascertained at once.

We contacted the remainder of the Lomonds, who were still climbing on the Cioch. A strong party of five of them undertook to make for the scene of the accident in an effort to locate the body that night. They took the climber with them, and arranged to split up and send word to us with all possible speed should the Pole be alive.

They had been climbing all day and had finished all their food, so that food was their greatest need should the search be prolonged. Nimlin and I arranged to go down to Glen Brittle with the ladies and the kiddie, get further help in case of need, and return up the mountain with food.

Thus we parted and hurried down to the glen. Glen Brittle House and hostel were warned and after a short time a stretcher-party turned out and started off up the hill. We had a quick meal, loaded up with a big supply of food, flasks, primus stove, etc., prepared for a night out and carried sufficient to feed the Lomonds.

About 10.30 p.m. we met the Lomonds at the mouth of Coire Lagan. They had ascended the Sgumain Stone Shoot, traversed to Bealach Coir' an Lochain, worked round rock and then saw a man lying clear on the screes below. One of them descended the rock and ascertained that the man was dead. He had fallen about five hundred feet, struck rock, bounded off, and landed on screes, receiving multiple injuries. Death must have been instantaneous. The speed and skill of this party cannot be too highly commended. The fact of their locating the body before darkness saved most of us a night out and an anxious and dangerous search. All of us returned to Glen Brittle.

Next day the urgency and the excitement had gone; there remained only the hard drudgery of stretcher work. There were few volunteers: only a party from Glen Brittle House and our own crowd—fourteen in all. With the stretcher we took the route up Coir' a' Ghrunnda and found the boiler-plate slabs a sore trial, then up to the bealach and down rock to the screes where the body lay. On the way up it was suggested we should return via Sgumain Stone Shoot, but the comparatively short distance on screes on the Coruisk side of the bealach convinced us that the much longer upward traverse of the Sgumain route would be difficult and indeed dangerous for a laden stretcher-party. To reach Bealach Coir' an Lochain we had to pull the stretcher up rock. Two long ropes in front and two behind, with two men manning each rope and the rest handling the stretcher. It was hard work and the whole party was required till we got down to the moor, from where we were able to have two good relays. Eventually we reached Glen Brittle about eight o'clock at night.

A sergeant and a constable had come over from Portree to make enquiries. As I had not been in Portree since the war, and as supplies were rather short at the hostel, I got a lift back in the police car. At half-past eleven on the Wednesday of Glasgow Fair week we got to Portree—a very dark night, raining hard and Portree packed to the roof. As I did not fancy hunting for accommodation at that time of night the sergeant very obligingly put me in a cell at the police station. I was surprised at such a modern prison up there. The cell was all stone, had a high arched roof, a small barred window high up, a peephole in the door, light controlled from outside, while even the blankets had red arrows on them.

I was dead tired after two full days on the hills and remember nothing more till the sergeant came into the cell at half-past nine the next morning with a mug of tea and a big slice of bread and jam. It was still raining. To get back to Glen Brittle I'd have had to take the bus to Sligachan, then walk for nine miles over Bealach a' Mhaim. Still rather tired and with a big load to carry such a prospect did not attract me, so I asked the sergeant if he knew of any vehicle going to Glen Brittle that day (for few cars venture over that awful road). The sergeant replied that a Portree man was going back for the body and that I could go with him.

I went off to do my shopping, bought a dozen pairs of kippers and much other stuff, and then located my man. What a shock I got! I had thought of a van or a truck, but here was a full-size hearse complete with coffin. I travelled the thirty-odd miles back to Glen Brittle sitting inside the hearse, holding on to the coffin with one hand and holding a dozen pairs of kippers in the other, which must indeed be something of the ultimate in hitch-hiking.

The Cuillin of Rhum were on our programme that year, but the weather broke and we were denied them. Next July we made great plans. We would arrive at Mallaig on a Thursday evening, have a moonlight sail to the Isle of Eigg in Sandy's boat. We would climb the Scuir of Eigg, camp on the island till MacBrayne's ship called on the Saturday, cross over to Rhum, camp there till the Tuesday, then cross over to the beloved Glen Brittle. It all sounded perfect, the more so when permission to camp on Rhum was obtained.

At Mallaig it was wet and stormy and a long journey by open motor-boat quite out of the question. We spent the night at the station and Eigg had to be scored off our schedule. Nothing but Rhum now by steamer on the Saturday morning, which meant one more night at Mallaig. A hotel?—not if you are with the Lomonds, who pride themselves on their ability to find or make a howff anywhere at any time. After some searching Dave Easson and myself got the use of a railwayman's hut half a mile up towards Morar, only to find that the others had gone one better and wangled a hut right on the pierhead, which was much more convenient, though it had a concrete floor. There we all bedded down and joined the *Loch Nevis* at 6 a.m. on the Saturday.

I should explain that I had obtained permission for *four* to camp on Rhum from the Saturday till the Tuesday. That delectable isle is something of a forbidden land: when others heard of my good fortune, they horned in, as good climbers will. Quite justifiably the keeper was rather annoyed as piles and piles of food and equipment went ashore and then eight people landed, accompanied by two babies and a pram. "But," he exclaimed, "you said only four!"

63. J. Banford on top of "Gendarme", west ridge of Sgurr nan Gillean. The ridge is narrow and shattered and daylight can be seen through it. It forms part of the main ridge traverse

64. W. H. Murray on the summit of Sgurr a' Ghreadaidh shortly after dawn (see text page 116). Coire Lagan is on the far side of the ridge and Sgurr Mhic Coinnich, Sgurr Thearlaich, Sgurr Alasdair and Sgurr Sgumain circle round it. The ridge to the Dubhs runs out to the left from Sgurr Thearlaich with Sgurr nan Eag in the background

65. After the great day (see page 118)

71. J. B. Nimlin and B. H. H. at Loch Coruisk. The photograph proves that trees grow there and that it is not the gloomy wilderness of bare rock so often described. Sgurr Dubh Beag in the background

72. About 2,000 feet up before we entered the mist when climbing Blaven. J. B. Nimlin stops for a smoke and looks down on Loch an Athain (see p. 127)

73. The Fluted Buttress of Sgurr Mhic Coinnich from Sgurr Coir' an Lochain. The chief climbs shown are:

A–A—Crack of Dawn

B–B—Fluted Buttress route

C–C—North-east Buttress

The North-east gully, climbed by O'Brien and Julian in 1912, is seen as a dark shadow between B and C, while the Inaccessible Pinnacle appears at the top right corner of photo

The keeper was greatly interested when I showed him a bottle of the Scottish Tourist Board's new midge-preventive, then on trial before being put on the market, for midges are the curse of Rhum as of Skye. He then asked me if I had anything for sheep-tick. We tested that lotion thoroughly and found it very effective. Tom Johnston ought surely to be the patron saint of campers, for campers were ever the worst sufferers from the midge. Never, in post-war camping, have the midges proved a menace, and it was Tom Johnston who set the scientists to the task of discovering the antidote. The Cuillin of Rhum delighted us. For the weekend we had them to ourselves and were content to ridge-walk.

On the Tuesday the MacDonalds of Soay kept their tryst and arrived with their motor-boat to take us over the sea to Skye. Seas were kind and we were regaled with stories of other days in Rhum: how, when a former proprietor kept a private zoo, an alligator escaped from the pond and made for the hills and how they organised an alligator hunt; of their recent success as film stars when they took part in a film on shark fishing; and of the somewhat cut-throat competition between themselves and the other Soay family in connection with motor-boat trips for visitors.

Glen Brittle again, to find further progress—Ewen MacRae had just started a regular bus service. If anyone deny enterprise to the Islefolk this be the proof of it. True, there are bridges where previously there were water-splashes, otherwise the road has not improved. It is doubtful if, in all Scotland, there is a regular bus service over such an awful road as this, and only a hero would have thought of starting one.

For us, on arrival, it was the same old story—a story becoming much too frequent in Skye—of how a tourist had left Sligachan without telling anyone where he was going and would we please join the search parties. He had already been missing for several days. No one knew whether he had taken the Glen Brittle or the Glen Sligachan path, whether he was likely to make for the corries or the tops. He might have been anywhere in thirty square miles. Had he left word of his route or taken the elementary precaution of carrying a whistle he would have been found at once. Hundreds took part in that search day after day.

We took our share and I can recall no pleasure in it. Even the weather was weeping when a party of eight of us combed Glen Sligachan, swung high up into Harta and Lota corries and circled round back to the glen. It was a long, hard day, for one must keep approximately at the same distance from one's neighbour and cannot choose the easiest route. Images of that day are blurred, but I do remember noting that each of the eight had different ideas as to the best outer garment for Cuillin rain. One wore an oilskin jacket, one an army tunic, one an air force tunic, one an anorak with hood, two, different types of climbers' jackets, one a waterproof sheet over a tweed jacket, while the eighth was the most conspicuous of the lot: he was clad in that yellow outfit supposed to be worn by shipwrecked mariners; while one could easily lose sight of the others that murky day he was always easily distinguishable as he kept his place at the end of the line high up on the hillside. The body of the tourist was found near the top of Drum Hain about a year later.

To recover from that work we had a long, quiet day at Rudha an Dunain, exploring the ruined castle and the prehistoric remains, building a raft on the inland loch and admiring the canal construction of the ancients.

The usual climbing around Coire Lagan followed; then someone suggested we draw a line on the map from Glen Brittle to Blaven and try to follow it. Its summit was almost due east of our camp and it would mean crossing two ridges to reach it. Though the weather was unsettled and we expected to be away for at least two days we did not bother carrying stoves, sleeping bags or a tent. We planned to start at 2 a.m., but, as is usual with climbers in Skye, it was about two hours later before we started up Coire na Banachdich.

No glamorous dawn greeted us, just a greyish light with mist on all the tops. From the bealach we started down towards Coruisk at once, for it was too cold to linger. At about fifteen hundred feet we sighted a rowan tree, surely about the highest in the Cuillin. It had a dead branch. That, with heather roots, meant a fire, a brew-up, a hearty breakfast and an hour's laze. We were in no hurry and dawdled down to the lochside, where a brief blink of sunshine induced us to loiter awhile and prove, by means of photographs, that even in such weather Loch Coruisk is not entirely a gloomy place. (No. 71.)

As we ascended to the summit of Drum Hain, black jagged peaks appeared momently through the mist; remotely high they looked, up there in a menacing sky. The menace was only too true. Lashing rain drove us down to Strath na Creitheach. It was now afternoon and we were twelve hours out—time for a meal! We found slight shelter outside a fisherman's hut, and I still think with relish of the substantial dinner we cooked over a wood fire. There was soup, two tins of M. and V. with mashed potatoes (made from powder, and a godsend to the camper), tea, bread, jam and cakes. After such a banquet we were ready for Blaven, even at six o'clock on a dull wet night. Luck was with us, for the rain stopped as we mounted upwards, enabling me to take a last photograph before we entered the regions of mists (No. 72). We had intended making for the col between Blaven and Clach Glas, but, in thick mist, strayed to the south and found a sporting ridge which led us dramatically to the summit of Blaven, just between its two peaks. It was 8 p.m. The true mountain worshipper ever receives his reward. We were again in that delectable land above the clouds. Now and then spear-points of rock appeared in the west, but it was Clach Glas, rising from the clouds like a great Alpine peak, which held our gaze. For a brief five minutes we actually saw down to Loch Slapin, though no distant views were ours.

I would fain have lingered on the summit, but the wind was rising and we had to seek shelter for the night. My idea was to get the use of a barn or outhouse at Camasunary but, says Jock, "Davie knows a howff." Apparently, in some previous wanderings, Davie had noticed a cave somewhere by Loch Scavaig which he *thought* he could find again and which could be made into a suitable shelter.

A long easy ridge led us downwards to the mouth of the river which drains from Loch na Creitheach to the sea, only to find the tide full and the stepping-stones covered. It was ten o'clock when we floundered across thigh-deep, then trekked round that awful path by the Bad Step to Coruisk once more. It was rapidly darkening. Where was that cave? Davie held on across the River Scavaig, past the Mad Burn and, at last, when we had begun to doubt its existence, found what was more a slit in the rocks than a cave. A bitter cold wind was blowing. Hurriedly we piled up stones and turf to form a windbreak at the entrance, gathered heather for bedding and driftwood from the shore and soon had a blazing fire a-going. That fire was needed, for it was a mighty cold night. Indeed, my memories of Skye of post-war years are of fires wherever we stopped on our wanderings, of John Nimlin's delight in beachcombing and the relics of torpedoed and mined ships which litter the shores of the island. Our fire was almost a bonfire for we had lugged up logs like railway sleepers, and at one moment it threatened to set our heather floor in a blaze.

I was dead tired and fell off to sleep. Some time during the night I woke up and noticed that Jock and Davie were sitting up crouched over the fire and obviously feeling very cold. As I was quite snug I was puzzled, but fell off to sleep again before I could work it out. When I woke up in broad daylight I had the cave to myself, and, on looking over the windbreak, found the other two cooking breakfast on an open fire outside. Tea was handed in, so that I had

127

breakfast in bed. I learned the solution of the overnight problem. In the hurry and darkness a hole in the back of the cave had gone unnoticed. All night the wind roared through, so that Jock and Dave felt like corks in a wind-tunnel and got but little sleep, while I had the luck to be out of line of the draught. That must be the exception which proves the rule that the last man into a howff gets the most uncomfortable berth.

The weather was still unsettled and the other two were keen on a rock climb in Coir' a' Ghrunnda on the way home. My boots, of pre-war vintage, were not in a state for such a standard of climbing, forbye I had not previously been on Gars-bheinn and there it was just above us. So we parted, they to go round by the coast, myself to travel back by the main ridge.

Having all day before me I took things very leisurely and did not start upwards till the afternoon. It was only when resting high up that I realised the force of the wind. My scarf blew away and disappeared into the void, while later my beret followed suit. I mourned for that beret: it had seen me over fifty Munros. On the ridge it was necessary, at times, to tack along one or other side, but this part of the ridge offers no difficulties. Once I briefly glimpsed a corrie to the west, all else was mist. Solo wandering is often condemned, but no one may truly know the mountains till he has travelled alone among them the day long. Perceptions are keener, there is a fine sense of freedom, idiosyncrasies of one's companions need no longer be studied. It was one of my slowest journeys and I have no regrets—why hurry, anyway? So I wandered happily along, often stopping to consult my map. I remembered the story of the party who had ascended from Loch Coruisk over the Dubhs in mist and descended to what they took to be Coir' a' Ghrunnda, only to find themselves coming out of the mist with Loch Coruisk in front of them. They had descended by Coir' an Lochain instead and to reach Glen Brittle had to make a long journey in darkness round the base of Gars-bheinn. In thick mist identification even of known places is not always easy and once one leaves the ridge one corrie may seem much like another.

My last sandwich I retained till I descended and glimpsed the lochan at the head of Coir' a' Ghrunnda. Here at least was a landmark of which I could be certain; now only the rough going in the lower corrie and a moorwalk. It was 8 p.m. when I reached Glen Brittle. I had been forty hours out.

Forty hours out for a brief half-hour on the summit of Blaven. Worth it?— a thousand times yes! For I, too, had gained the Treasure of the Cuillin.

128

Envoi

SKYE has prospered in the years since the end of the World War. The brave experiment of the Skye Week in 1950 was a brilliant success and focussed world attention on the little island. Quite rightly it is now to be an annual function.

Everywhere there are signs of new vigour, more fields under cultivation, more cattle on the hills and experiments in grassland management in conjunction with the Board of Agriculture. The Storr lochs have been harnessed and hydro-electric and Forestry Commission schemes provide employment for many. Roads have been improved, but still the road to Glen Brittle is as bad as ever. Surely something will be done to improve it soon, for the Cuillin bring thousands to Skye.

In Sligachan and Glen Brittle the old generation has passed away. The old names remain and a younger generation carries on the tradition of kindliness, hospitality and good cooking, well understanding the vagaries of the climbers.

New climbs continue to be done, standards are being pushed higher and higher. Sron na Ciche is still the magnet and is now criss-crossed with routes. Most of them are shown in photograph No. 34, but it was not possible to show them all. This is not intended to be a guide, merely to show the great number of routes.

There is now a "Crack of Doom", a "Doom Flake" and "Integrity", all in the severe class. When Ian Allan made a new route up the Cioch slab in 1944 there were doubters who would not believe it, just as happened with the Waterpipe Gully climb fifty years previously. Allan settled the matter by climbing it again scratching arrows with a bit of rock as he went, hence the name Arrow route. There was a new central buttress route in 1951, while

"Cioch Grooves" (also 1951) is notable for the fact that it was the first climb in Skye in which a piton was used for direct progress. One hopes this precedent will not be followed.

Other new routes are on Sgurr a' Mhadaidh, Sgurr Dearg and Sgurr a' Ghreadaidh, while a girdle traverse of the South Crag of Coir' a' Ghrunnda face of Sgurr Sgumain was made by E. Wood Johnson and Ernest Wiggin in 1947.

All these new ways are near older routes; it was not till recently that a complete new climbing area was discovered. Or rather, it was in the nature of a rediscovery, as Conor O'Brien and E. L. Julian made a gully climb on the Coireachan Ruadha face of Sgurr Mhic Coinnich as long ago as 1912. No further exploration was made till 1949, though the great buttress which falls from the summit of Sgurr Mhic Coinnich to that corrie must have been seen by hundreds of ridge walkers and those going from Glen Brittle to Loch Coruisk via Bealach Coire na Banachdich. The superlative attractions of Sron na Ciche and its nearness to Glen Brittle would account for this neglect.

The climbing done there since 1949 is assuredly the most notable climbing in the Cuillin during the last quarter-century. Two young Aberdeen climbers, Bill Brooker and Douglas Sutherland, attempted to climb the buttress in that year, but were defeated. In 1950 Brooker was joined by C. M. Dixon, a young Leeds climber. After several failures they won through to success by making the first ascent of the Fluted Buttress, involving seven hundred feet of continuously difficult climbing, and later made other two routes on the same face.

In 1951 the same two returned to Skye, confident that the "back" of Sgurr Mhic Coinnich had still more to offer. They were not disappointed and made the first ascent of a magnificent route to which they gave the equally magnificent name of the "Crack of Dawn", a climb of very severe standard. Altogether five new routes have been made by this pair and now that the way has been shown other routes and variations will certainly follow (No. 73). No pitons were used, proof enough that there are still many possibilities among the crags of Skye without resorting to artificial aids. True, such aids are increasingly used elsewhere, but should we not leave unsullied this, our Cragsman's Paradise?

The Scottish Mountaineering Club's Guide to Skye is now quite out of date and a new one in the style of the pocket guide to Glencoe is at present being prepared. Its publication will certainly lead to intensified climbing in the Cuillin and further new routes.

Envoi

Must progress in climbing always be reckoned in new climbs? Should it not be judged by the increasing numbers who are able to look after themselves on the hills?

I close my eyes and imagine myself on the hillside near Glen Brittle post office. There is a blaze of gorse by the river, cattle are browsing in lush green fields; beyond, the brown moor rises up to lighter scree and the black-brown peaks.

A moving trail winds up the hillside. Old and young, male and female, wearing big boots and old clothes and carrying ropes, cameras and food, they disappear from the lower world till darkness and hunger bring them home at night. The beginners take the easy ways or picnic in the corries, the more experienced make for the ridges, while the *tigers* test nerve and sinew on the hardest routes. From Sligachan, too, there will be a similar trail.

Where once there were but a few pilgrims now thousands seek—and find—the Treasure of the Cuillin.

Sources

PRINTED SOURCES

1544 *Description of the Western Isles of Scotland* – Sir Donald Munro
1654 *The Yle of Skye* – Timothy Pont
1703 *A Description of the Western Islands of Scotland* – Martin Martin
1746 *Lyon in Mourning* – Malcolm MacLeod
1772 *A Tour in Scotland* – Thomas Pennant
1775 *Journey to the Western Islands of Scotland* – Samuel Johnson
1785 *Journal of a Tour to the Hebrides* – James Boswell
1800 *Mineralogy of Scotland* – Robert Jamieson
1814 *Scenery of the Grampian Mountains* – G. F. Robson
1815 *The Lord of the Isles* – Sir Walter Scott
1819 *A Description of the Western Islands* – John MacCulloch
1838 *The Life of Sir Walter Scott* – J. G. Lockhart
1838 *Journal of a Tour in Scotland* – C. Lesingham Smith
1842 *Circuit Journeys* – Lord Cockburn
1846 *Geology of the Cuillin Hills* – J. D. Forbes
1850 *Autumnal Rambles* – Thos. Grierson
1852 *Household Words* – Charles Dickens
1853 *Norway and its Glaciers* – J. D. Forbes
1859 *Blackwood's Magazine*
1860 *Three Months in the Highlands* – C. R. Weld
1862 *Blackwood's Magazine*
1865 *A Summer in Skye* – Alexander Smith
1872 *Scotsman* – articles by Nicolson
1873 *Modern Painters* – John Ruskin
1875 *Good Words* – Nicolson
1883 *The Hebrid Isles* – Robert Buchanan
1885 *Rambles in Skye* – Malcom Ferguson
1893 *Daily Telegraph*
1895 *Cornhill Magazine*
1895 *The Field*
1898 *Graphic*
1908 *Rock Climbing in Skye* – A. P. Abraham
1908 *The Misty Isle of Skye* – J. A. MacCulloch
1923 *Guide to Skye* – S.M.C.
1933 *Tramping in Skye* – B. H. Humble
1934 *Mountain Days in the Isle of Skye* – J. E. B. Wright
1934 *The Songs of Skye* – B. H. Humble
1950 *Undiscovered Scotland* – W. H. Murray
1951 *A Progress in Mountaineering* – J. H. B. Bell

Appendix

CONQUERING OF THE CUILLIN

1836   Sgurr nan Gillean – Professor Forbes
1845   Bruach na Frithe – Professor Forbes
1857   Blaven – Professor Nicol and Algernon Swinburne
1859   Sgurr na Stri – C. R. Weld
1870   Sgurr a' Ghreadaidh – W. Tribe and John Mackenzie
1873   Sgurr na Banachdich – Alexander Nicolson
1873   Sgurr Dearg – ?
1873   Sgurr Alasdair – Alexander Nicolson
1874   Sgurr Dubh Mor – Alexander Nicolson
1880   Inaccessible Pinnacle – Charles and Lawrence Pilkington
1880   Bidein Druim nan Ramh (North top) – W. W. Naismith
1883   Bidein Druim nan Ramh (main top) – L. Pilkington, E. Hulton and J. Heelis
1887   Sgurr Mhic Coinnich – C. Pilkington's party
1887   Sgurr Thearlaich – C. Pilkington's party
1887   Sgurr na h-Uamha – C. Pilkington's party
1887   Clach Glas – C. Pilkington's party
1889   Basteir Tooth – Collie
1896   Sgurr Coir' an Lochain – Collie, Howell, Naismith and Mackenzie

STRAIGHTENING OUT

1886   Inaccessible Pinnacle Traverse – A. H. Stocker and A. G. Parker
1891   Thearlaich-Dubh gap – W. W. King, N. Collie and J. Mackenzie
1898   King's Chimney, Sgurr Mhic Coinnich – W. W. King, W. N. Naismith and W. Douglas
1898   Basteir Tooth – W. N. Naismith and A. M. Mackay

TRAVERSE

1911   First traverse of main ridge – L. G. Shadbolt and A. C. MacLaren
1920   First solo traverse of main ridge – Howard Somervell
1926   First woman does the traverse – Dr M. M. Barker (with C. D. Frankland)
1928   First all-women's party – L. Bray, T. and B. Wells
1939 (June)   First traverse of main ridge plus Blaven – I. G. Charleson and W. E. Forde
1939 (July)   All Skye Munros climbed in one day – F. B. Dutton-Walker, J. K. Cooke, F. McGavin
1944   First solo traverse of main ridge plus Blaven and Clach Glas – J. M. Edwards

THE GREAT TRAVERSE

(Only a few specimen times are given here

	L. G. Shadbolt / A. C. MacLaren (S.M.C.) June 1911	T. H. Somervell (S.M.C.) June 1920	J. H. B. Bell (S.M.C.) / F. S. Smythe (Y.R.) July 1924	B. R. Goodfellow / F. Yates (Rucksack Club) July 1924	Miss M. M. Barker (Pinnacle Club), C. D. Frankland August 1926	Miss L. Bray (P.C.) / Misses T and B. Wells May 1928	Peter Bicknell (Alpine Club) August 1932
Glen Brittle	3.35 a.m.	7.11 a.m.	5.15 a.m.	11.47 p.m.	Scavaig Hut	2.30 a.m.	4.30 a.m.
Gars-bheinn	6.7	9.16	7.53–8.23	9.40	5.00 a.m.		6.3
Sgurr nan Eag	6.50	9.58	8.58				7.32–7.47
Sgurr Dubh na Dà Bheinn	7.45	10.41	9.43				8.10
Bealach Coir' an Lochain	7.55–8.20			7.15			
Sgurr Alasdair	9	11.43	10.50	5.50			9
Sgurr Thearlaich	9.7	11.50	10.57				9.5
Sgurr Mhic Coinnich	9.50	12.18 p.m.	11.45				9.26
Inaccessible Pinnacle	10.55	1.17	12.33–12.47 p.m.	3.50			10.2–10.22
Sgurr Dearg	11.15–12	1.25–2.11	1.10 p.m.				
Sgurr na Banachdich	12.30 p.m.	2.40	1.41	2.30 p.m.			10.55
Sgurr Thormaidh	12.42		1.56				11.8
Sgurr a' Ghreadaidh	1.7–1.20	3.32	2.21	↑			11.25
Sgurr a' Mhadaidh	1.40	3.50	(40 min. rest)				11.51
Bidein Druim nan Ramh	2.40–3.20	4.42–5	4.20	11.30 a.m.			12.40–1 p.m.
Bruach na Frithe	4.45		5.34			9 p.m.–3.30a.m.	2.7 p.m.
Sgurr a' Fionn Choire	4.50	6.13	5.50	10.12 a.m.			2.15–2.20
Bealach na Lice	5–5.30	6.20–6.50					
Am Basteir	6	7.21	6.30				2.40
Sgurr nan Gillean	6.25	7.45	7.3	8.50 a.m.	8.30 p.m.	9 a.m.	3.4
Sgurr na h-Uamha		8.5			Scavaig Hut		Pinnacle Rid
Sligachan	8.20 p.m.	9.29 p.m.	9.26	6.55 a.m.	1 a.m.	11 a.m.	
Glen Brittle							4.27 p.m.
Ridge time	12 hr. 18 min.	10 hr. 39 min.	11 hr. 10 min.	11 hr. 10 min.	14 hr. (approx.)	30 hr. (approx.)	8 hr. 1 min.

Others who have done the Great Traverse are :

Pre-War

E. H. Sale; J. D. Brown; B. R. Goodfellow; A. S. Bullough; R. A. Hodgkin; F. A. Pullinger; J. P. Cooper; J. Higginbothan; D. G. Ritson; H. B. Rowntree; G. G. Macphee; J. C. S. Ewen; J. F. Hamilton; J. A. H. Peacocke; D. G. Hodgkinson; G. G. Macphee; R. W. Lovel.

Post-War

D. Angus; J. Henderson; Ian Potter; D. J. Horn; J. S. Huddort; J. H. S. Watson; P. R. Charworth-Masters; J. Robertson; G. H. Francis; A. G. M. Flew; C. Yorgenson; P. Lloyd; Edwin Holt; E. Jones; D. Edmiston.

Plus of course those who have included it in the Greater Traverse.

PARTIES AND TIMES

Many other parties have done the ridge)

F. Broadbent T. F. Broadbent July 1936	J. H. B. Bell C. M. Allan (S.M.C.) June 1935	W. H. Murray J. Banford (J.M.C.S.) June 1937	E. G. H. Kempson J. C. Lloyd C. G. Wylie April 1938	W. L. Woods Miss Hudson (17) June 1940	S. Fry L. Greenwood A. Thomas (Climbers' Club) June 1946	C. B. Machin E. Lloyd D. Stevens (Midland Assoc. Mntns.) June 1948	D. D. Stewart (E.U.M.C.) July 1950	G. C. Band (C.U.M.C.) Aug. 1950	Jack Boag Barbara Cole (M.A.M.) June 1951
6.40 a.m. 9.20–9.25	2. a.m. 4.30 a.m.	3.30–4	4 a.m. 7	2.5 a.m. 5 a.m.	Glen Brittle to	7.30 a.m. 10.30	12.45 p.m.	start Camasunary 10 a.m.	4.05 a.m. 7.20 a.m.
10.5 10.52–11	+ Sgurr Dubh Mor + Sgurr Sgumain	4.40 5.23–5.53 6.40	7.37 8.28 9.11 9.38		Glen Brittle 18½ hours 12 hours on ridge	1.30 p.m.			8.45 10.15 12 noon 12.8 p.m. 12.50
11.55 12.25 p.m. 1.16 1.33 2.7 2.15 2.46 2.57–3.5		7.25 8.30–9 9.50 10 10.31 11	10.19 11.00 11.20 12 noon 12.13 p.m. 12.31 p.m. 12.57 p.m.			3.35 p.m. 5 6 7 8		2.37 p.m.	2.5–3.5 2.45 4.9 4.45 5.45
4.35 5.40 5.55	2.15 p.m.	12.7–12.40 p.m. 2.5 2.30–3	2.12 3.27 3.31				5.30 p.m.		6.50 9.10 9.35
6.30 6.58	5.14 p.m.	3.40 4.20	4.39 5.5	8 p.m.		12 Midnight	7.30 p.m.	5.20 p.m.	10.20 11.3
7.40 9.35	9.15 p.m.		7.30 p.m.	12 Midnight		3 a.m.	9.30 p.m.	Camasunary 9.45 p.m.	2.20 a.m.
9 hr. 38 min.	12 hr. 44 min.	11 hr. 50 min.	10 hr. 5 min.	15 hr.	12 hr.	13 hr. 30 min.	6 hr. 45 min. (approx.)	7 hr. 20 min. (approx.)	15 hr. 43 min.

THE GREATER TRAVERSE: TIMES AND PARTIES

	I. C. Charleson W. E. Forde June 1939	F. B. Dutton-Walker J. K. Cooke F. McGavin } Wayfarers' Club July 1939	W. H. Murray R. G. Donaldson } J.M.C.S. August 1939	J. M. Edwards (Climbers' Club) June 1944	S. Thomson (Yorkshire Ramblers) August 1944
Camp (Glen Sligachan)		8 p.m.			
Camp (foot of Gars-bheinn)	1.30 a.m.				
Glen Brittle		6.10 p.m.	9.30 p.m.	8.30 a.m.	4.50 a.m.
Gars-bheinn	3–5		2 a.m.		7.20
Sgurr Dubh na Da Bheinn	4.36	+ Sgurr Dubh Mor and Sgurr Sgumain			
Sgurr Alasdair	5.30				8.55
Sgurr Mhic Coinnich	6.45				
Sgurr Dearg	8–8.30	2 p.m.	7–7.35		10.5–10.10
Sgurr a' Ghreadaidh	9.50				
Bidein Druim nan Ramh	11.40–12.8 p.m.		10.6–10.36		12.50–1.5 p.m.
Bruach na Frithe	1.45				
Sgurr nan Gillean	3.28–3.35	9 p.m.	1.30 p.m.		3–3.20
Camp (Glen Sligachan)	5.30–6.45				
Clach Glas		10 p.m.	8		
Blaven	11.5 p.m.	11.40 p.m.	9	11 p.m.	7
Camp (Glen Sligachan)	1.25 a.m.		1 a.m.		
Glen Brittle				8.30 a.m.	1.10 a.m.
Ridge time	20 hr.	23 hr.	19 hr.	approx. 12 hr. 30 min.	11 hr. 40 min.

Index

Index

Index

Index

Sgurr a' Fhionn Choire, 7, 61, 89
Sgurr a' Ghreadaidh, 5, 42, 47, 53, 55, 61, 65, 87, 93, 97, 116, 130
Sgurr a' Mhadaidh, 5, 42, 49, 53, 55, 61, 65, 75, 83, 86, 87, 91, 94, 116, 117, 130
Sgurr Alasdair, xiii, 5, 29, 41, 42, 43, 53, 55, 59, 61, 68, 75, 80, 84, 88, 97, 107, 110, 114, 115, 118, 120, 121, 122
Sgurr an Fheadain, 5, 71, 75
Sgurr Coir' an Lochain, 7, 55, 61
Sgurr Dearg, 5, 28, 39, 41, 42, 53, 55, 60, 75, 92, 93, 95, 97, 109, 121, 130
Sgurr Dubh Beag, 6, 36, 68
Sgurr Dubh Mor, 5, 23, 28, 33, 46, 53, 64, 68, 94, 97, 98, 118
Sgurr Dubh na Da Bheinn, 5, 22, 46, 87, 118
Sgurr Sgumain, 5, 29, 41, 43, 59, 80, 84, 85, 94, 97, 98, 114, 115, 121, 130
Sgurr Mhic Coinnich, 5, 41, 42, 46, 53, 59, 66, 87, 88, 93, 114, 121, 122, 130
Sgurr na Banachdich, 5, 18, 28, 42, 53, 87, 90, 95, 115, 116.
Sgurr na Gobhar, 23
Sgurr na h-Uamha, 5, 41, 46, 61, 85, 90, 93, 96, 98
Sgurr na Stri, 6, 18, 36, 65
Sgurr nan Eag, 6, 84, 87
Sgurr nan Gillean, 3, 5, 17, 18, 20, 22, 26, 27, 35, 39, 41, 47, 49, 52, 55, 59, 61, 64, 67, 77, 82, 84, 87, 90, 92, 93, 95, 98, 108, 112, 116, 120

Sgurr Thearlaich, 5, 41, 42, 43, 46, 53, 66, 68, 86, 87, 88, 114, 115, 121
Sgurr Thormaid, 5, 87, 116
Shadbolt, Leslie, 81, 83, 87, 90, 92
Simmonds, B. H., 98
Sligachan, xiii, 15, 20, 25, 32, 34, 38, 47, 48, 49, 53, 54, 55, 57, 59, 64, 68, 70, 73, 77, 87, 91, 92, 94, 96, 97, 98, 99, 101, 102, 106, 108, 109, 111, 112, 120, 125, 129, 131
Slingsby, W. C., 42, 43, 68, 70, 83
Smith, Alexander, 23
Smith, Lesingham, 15, 16, 17, 20, 21
Smythe, F. S., 79, 85, 91, 104
Soay, 63, 106, 118
Solly, Godfrey, 68, 70, 79
Somervell, T. H., 79, 90, 91, 92, 94, 96
Sron na Ciche, 55, 56, 77, 79, 81, 83, 84, 85, 104, 105, 109, 114, 115, 120, 129
Steeple, E. W., 78, 79, 81, 84
Stewart, Dan, 95
Stocker, A. H., 40, 41, 47, 52
Storr, xiv, 111
Strath na Creitheach, 126
Stuart, Charles Edward, 9, 34
Sutherland, Douglas, 130
Sutherland family, 103
Swan, Cameron, 46
Swinburne, Algernon, 21
Symmons, G. R., 94

Tatham, H. F. W., 46
Thearlaich-Dubh Gap, 55, 64, 66, 87, 88, 91, 93, 98, 106
Thomson, J. M. Archer, 81

Thomson, R. E., 73
Thomson, Sydney, 95, 99, 100
Tomset, R., 98
Tribe, W., 47
Turner, J. M. W., 14, 15, 38

Unna, P. J. H., 78, 79

Valentine, Sheriff, 53

Wakefield, A. W., 86
Walker, F. B. Dutton, 97
Walker, Horace, 40, 41, 42, 70, 109
Walker, H., 68, 79
Ward, Michael, 99
Waterpipe Gully 61, 71, 73, 74, 90, 129
Wayfarers' Club, 70, 97
Wedderburn, E. A. M., 119
Wedderburn, T. M., 120
Weld, C. R., 21, 23, 25, 60
Wells, T. and B., 93
Whymper, E. 59, 108
Wicks, J. H., 59
Wilding, J., 84
Williams, Alfred, 38, 43, 62, 63
Willink brothers, 21
Wilson, Dr Claude, 69
Wilson, Graham, 90, 104
Wilson, John, 18
Window Buttress, 55, 115, 120
Wood, W. L., 95
Wooley, Herman, 42, 70
Wright, J. E. B., 76, 103

Yorkshire Ramblers, 70
Young, Geoffrey, Winthrop 82, 87

The Cuillin of Skye

Glen Brittle

LOCH SCAVAIG